Careers in Health Care

2006 Edition

WetFeet Insider Guide

Genevieve

Helping you make smarter career decisions.

WetFeet, Inc.

The Folger Building
101 Howard Street
Suite 300
San Francisco, CA 94105

Phone: (415) 284-7900 or 1-800-926-4JOB
Fax: (415) 284-7910
Website: www.WetFeet.com

Careers in Health Care

2006 Edition
ISBN: 1-58207-533-6

Photocopying Is Prohibited

Table of Contents

Health Care At a Glance

Opportunity Overview

- Because the Baby Boom generation is reaching retirement age these days—and because, as America's most well-off generation, the Baby Boomers have plenty of money to spend on health care as they get older and more frail—there are going to be an increasing number of career opportunities in the health-care sector for the next decade and possibly beyond.

- Health care practitioners include everyone from doctors, emergency medical technicians, and physical therapists to physician assistants, radiology technologists, respiratory therapists, nurses, home health aides, optometrists, podiatrists, and speech pathologists.

- The industry also employs a whole host of other types of workers—everyone from techies with expertise in health-care enterprise IT issues, to business, sales and marketing, and administrative types, to public policy workers, to medical writers, editors, and transcribers, to clinical research lab workers (the folks who do things like develop and conduct procedures like Pap smears and cholesterol tests).

- Employers in this industry include hospitals; managed-care providers; long-term and home-care providers; clinical research labs; specialty providers like nursing homes, diabetes care providers, and MRI clinics; and other health-care providers.

Major Pluses about Careers in Health Care

- You get to work for the good of others and society. Especially if you're in a career with regular patient contact, you get validation that, yes, your job has meaning.

- The pay can be good. While it's true that people in jobs like home health aide sometimes make not much more than minimum wage, becoming a doctor is usually still well worth it from a financial standpoint, and folks like nurses and medical technicians are in such high demand that they can do reasonably well, too.

- Because of the high demand for their services these days, nurses and some other health-care professionals often enjoy flexibility in terms of work hours.

Major Minuses about Careers in Health Care

- Increasingly, the business side of health care has come between patients and providers. "At my hospital, we're supposed to call the patients 'customers'," says one insider. "I keep telling my boss this is not Lord & Taylor! . . . All I can say is it stinks, and corporate America has no business in the system," says another.

- Because of staffing shortages, people in nursing are finding themselves saddled with increasing numbers of patients to care for. In some organizations today, nurses are under significant pressure to work overtime.

- The inequities in the U.S. health-care system can be frustrating and demoralizing. Insiders readily acknowledge the fact that the poor receive a different standard of health care from others in the United States.

Recruiting Overview

The recruiting process in health care varies by organization, job function, and career stage. Smaller health care providers—for example, the office of a family practice doctor—don't really do much in terms of recruiting, other than placing help-wanted ads in the window when they need new bodies. Larger organizations are more likely to have more formal recruiting programs and processes.

Because this is such a huge industry, employing so many different kinds of workers, there's no such thing as typical requirements for health-care job candidates. But in many cases—consider MDs and RNs—health-care workers must undergo a very specific course of education. And many health-care workers require specialized training and/or licensure or certification.

Still, there are a number of personal attributes that will probably make you a more attractive candidate for many health-care jobs:

- A desire to serve others. At its heart, despite the industry's shift in focus during the past generation from health-care quality to financial performance, in most practitioner jobs in the industry, it's all about helping patients. If it was just about the paycheck, health-care workers would look for work in industries with greater pay for less time and hassle.

- Some business sense. Still and all, the fact remains that most health-care organizations are more focused on the bottom line these days than ever. If you can show you understand the business reasons for the strategic and tactical decisions your potential employer makes, you'll be more likely to get the job.

- Grace under pressure. A lot of practitioner jobs count an ability to deal with stress, and an ability to make decisions on the fly, among the skills required for the job.

The Industry

Overview

The Bottom Line

Industry Breakdown

Industry Trends

Picking and Choosing

Overview

In the United States, health care is an industry in crisis. Where once the country's health-care system was the envy of the rest of the world—with the finest facilities and most innovative care options around—today U.S. health-care quality pales in comparison to health care in many other countries. Indeed, among the 24 industrialized nations making up the Organization for Economic Cooperation and Development, today the United States ranks only 16th in terms of female life expectancy, 17th in terms of male life expectancy, and 21st in terms of infant mortality rates. There have been great strides made in medical techniques and technologies in the past few decades, but today, many Americans can't afford access to those innovations. Fully 45 million Americans don't have health insurance, and many more only have disaster insurance. Even if you have a full-time job, there's a good chance your employer doesn't offer insurance that's affordable for you. If you belong to an HMO, you can only visit doctors who are part of the HMO's network. If you have to have an expensive procedure, chances are good that your insurance plan will make it as difficult as possible for you to get the plan's approval for that procedure. If approved, that procedure might take place at a non-hospital clinic rather than at a hospital—and even if it takes place at a hospital, they'll discharge you from the hospital much more quickly than they would have a generation ago. And health-care costs continue to skyrocket, meaning health insurance keeps getting more and more expensive.

Still, because the U.S. health-care industry is enormous (this is the largest industry in the United States, and health-care spending currently accounts for 15 percent of the country's Gross National Product), it employs many, many Americans—13.5 million, according to the U.S. Department of Labor's Bureau of Labor Statistics (BLS). And as the Baby Boomers retire and need more and more health-care services in coming years, the number of people employed in health care is expected to drastically increase;

indeed, according to the BLS, the number of jobs in the industry will grow by more than 27 percent between 2004 and 2014.

There is an enormous range of job opportunities in the medical and health-care industry—hundreds of different occupations to choose from in both health-care practice and business-oriented occupations.

Health care practitioners include everyone from doctors, emergency medical technicians, and physical therapists to physician assistants, radiology technologists, respiratory therapists, nurses, home health aides, optometrists, podiatrists, and speech pathologists. If you're interested in healing people and keeping them healthy, there's almost certainly a job for you somewhere in the health-care industry.

The industry also employs a whole host of other types of workers—everyone from techies with expertise in health-care enterprise IT issues, to business, sales and marketing, and administrative types, to public policy workers, to medical writers, editors, and transcribers, to clinical research lab workers (the folks who do things like develop and conduct procedures like Pap smears and cholesterol tests). And the industry's even bigger if, like some observers, you define it to include manufacturers of medical equipment and pharmaceutical and biotechnology companies in addition to hospitals, managed-care providers, long-term and home-care providers, clinical research labs, specialty providers like nursing homes, diabetes care providers, MRI clinics, and other health-care providers. There's no doubt about it: This industry is big-time, and the source of a dizzying array of career opportunities.

The Bottom Line

Thanks to the aging U.S. populace, in a few years the percentage of people over 50 years of age will be higher than it has ever been. That, plus the growth of the population as a whole, means there'll be tremendous job growth in almost all areas of health care, for everyone from executives to IT types to health care practitioners. The number of jobs in the industry will grow by more than a quarter over the next decade. According to the BLS, the job-growth rate will be especially strong for chiropractors, physician assistants, registered nurses, dental hygienists, medical records and health information technicians, home health aides, physical therapist assistants and aides, dental assistants, medical assistants, and personal and home care aides, among others.

Many health-care practitioner careers require licensing and at least some formal training. For example, each U.S. state requires doctors to be licensed by the state to practice in that state. Licenses are granted to graduates of accredited medical schools who have passed a licensing exam (the USMLE, United States Medical Licensing Examination) and completed 1 to 7 years of graduate medical school (residency) in an accredited program. Most specialists also become board certified in their specialty in order to gain an edge in a competitive job market, though board certification is not a state requirement.

Registered nurses (RNs) make up the largest health-care profession; there are approximately 2 million working RNs. Registered nurses play an important role in helping patients and do a wide range of work in clinical settings. RNs often work with physicians, but may also work alone on certain aspects of patient care.

In terms of compensation, the health-care industry offers the gamut—everything from careers like cardiovascular surgeon (average salary: $233K to $466K), at the high end, to home health aide (average salary: high teens to low 20s), at the low end.

Industry Breakdown

HOSPITALS

Despite the increased outsourcing of medical-records management, housekeeping, lab testing, and clinical services (e.g., orthopedics and radiology), hospitals remain the biggest employers in the health-care industry. The huge networks such as HCA and Tenet demand a steady supply of doctors, nurses, administrators, medical technicians, therapists, and other support staff. In areas where competition from HMOs is mounting and cost-cutting is a priority, former staff may move outside the immediate confines of a hospital. However, close and important links remain—particularly for any type of surgery or specialized treatment such as chemotherapy.

More than 5 million people are employed by hospitals nationwide. In fact, hospitals represent the second-largest source of private-sector jobs (after restaurants). Employees include health-care practitioners as well as IT, operations, administrative, and other staff.

Top 20 Hospital Systems

Hospital	2004 Revenue ($M)	1-Year Growth Rate (%)	Employees
Kaiser Permanente*	25,300	12.4	147,000
HCA	23,502	7.8	191,400
Adventist Health System*	10,123	20.0	44,000
Tenet Healthcare Corp.	9,919	−24.9	91,633
Ascension Health*	9,054	18.1	87,469
NewYork-Presbyterian Healthcare System*	7,060	7.3	53,562
Catholic Health Initiatives	6,121	0.8	53,549
Catholic Health East*	5,700	14.0	43,000
Sutter Health*	5,672	15.0	41,000
Catholic Healthcare West	5,397	8.2	40,000
Trinity Health	5,287	6.7	44,100
Mayo Foundation for Medical Education and Research*	4,822	9.0	42,620
Partners HealthCare System	4,561	8.1	n/a
Triad Hospitals	4,450	15.1	38,600
New York City Health and Hospitals Corp.*	4,200	−2.3	n/a
Universal Health Services	3,938	8.1	37,000
Providence Health System*	3,780	7.1	32,526
Community Health Systems	3,333	17.6	31,100
Intermountain Health Care*	3,267	14.7	n/a
Health Management Associates	3,206	25.2	28,000

*2003 figures.
Sources: Hoover's; WetFeet analysis.

HMOS AND PPOS

HMOs and preferred provider organizations (PPOs) are hybrids—basically a cross between a hospital and an insurance company. An HMO is a prepaid health plan delivering comprehensive care to members through designated providers. A PPO (Preferred Provider Organization) consists of a network of providers offering health-care services at a special network rate; PPO members can go to doctors outside the PPO network, but are charged a higher rate if they do so. Almost 30 percent of all persons in the United States are enrolled in one of the many HMOs and PPOs in the United States.

Both types of managed-care plans cover primary care visits, preventative services, and copayments for prescription drugs. Some of the largest organizations employ their own medical staffs and operate their own facilities where they treat patients; smaller ones may instead offer access to networks of private providers and hospitals. Competition among organizations in this arena is fierce—with mergers and acquisitions and internal strife often destabilizing the job market. Coventry, Humana, Harvard Pilgrim Health Care, Group Health Cooperative, and PacifiCare (one of the leading Medicare HMOs) are a few of the better-known players. Kaiser Foundation, based in Oakland, California, was the first HMO in the nation. HMO and PPO employees include health-care practitioners as well as IT, operations, administrative, and other staff.

Top HMOs/PPOs

HMO/PPO	2004 Revenue ($M)	1-Year Growth Rate (%)	Employees
Centers for Medicare & Medicaid Services*	453,000	−1.8	4,586
Blue Cross and Blue Shield Association	238,900	10.2	150,000
UnitedHealth Group	37,218	29.1	40,000
Kaiser Foundation Health Plan*	25,300	12.4	54,300
WellPoint	20,815	24.1	38,000
Aetna	19,904	10.7	26,700
CIGNA Corp.	18,176	−3.4	28,600
Blue Cross Blue Shield of Michigan*	13,716	9.6	8,500
Humana	13,104	7.2	13,700
PacifiCare Health Systems	12,277	11.5	9,800
Health Net	11,646	5.3	8,569
Highmark	9,118	12.0	11,000
Health Care Service Corp.*	8,190	12.0	13,000
The Regence Group*	6,700	7.2	6,000
Blue Shield of California*	6,203	34.1	4,200
Blue Cross and Blue Shield of Florida*	5,991	4.9	9,200
Blue Cross and Blue Shield of Minnesota*	5,984	19.4	3,500
WellChoice	5,827	8.3	5,400
Coventry Health Care	5,357	17.0	10,280
Horizon Blue Cross Blue Shield of New Jersey*	5,082	24.0	4,600

*2003 figures.
Sources: Hoover's; WetFeet analysis.

SPECIALTY PROVIDERS

As hospitals have attempted to cut costs, they have turned to firms that can provide specialized services at rock-bottom prices. These include everything from nursing homes (Beverly Enterprises), home infusion therapy providers (Apria Healthcare), kidney dialysis centers (DaVita), and diabetes treatment providers (American Healthways) to drug and alcohol rehabilitation clinics, blood banks, fertility clinics, and on and on and on.

Clinics that focus on special treatments such as chemotherapy, MRI and other scanning techniques, and physical therapy for the handicapped are also proliferating. Although most are small and locally run, Gambro (based in Sweden) and Fresenius Medical Care (based in Germany), two of the world's largest dialysis services companies, are focusing more attention on the national reach of their services. Gambro recently sold its U.S. services to DaVita. Other large organizations like these will undoubtedly emerge as their popularity increases.

The range of jobs available in this sector is broad. Everyone from nurses and doctors to medical technicians, mental health workers, and business types can find a home in the specialty-provider sector.

Top Specialty Providers

Specialty Provider	2004 Revenue ($M)	1-Year Growth Rate (%)	Employees
Fresenius Medical Care AG	6,228	12.7	44,526
Gambro AB	4,025	11.6	21,279
DaVita	2,299	14.0	15,300
US Oncology*	1,966	19.0	8,096
Specialized Care Services	1,878	24.5	n/a
Magellan Health Services	1,795	18.8	4,300
Accredo Health	1,475	10.3	2,491
Renal Care Group	1,345	33.8	8,603
Ardent Health Services*	1,320	223.5	10,100
FHC Health Systems*	1,300	9.4	8,198
Lincare Holdings	1,269	10.6	7,857
Concentra	1,102	4.9	10,370
MedCath Corp.	693	27.6	4,374
America Service Group	665	21.1	7,430
Hanger Orthopedic Group	569	3.8	3,227
Dialysis Clinic	547	n/a	5,000
Psychiatric Solutions	487	65.9	9,100
Alliance Imaging	432	4.0	2,083
Vitas Healthcare Corp.*	420	n/a	6,500
United Surgical Partners International	390	−8.8	3,450

*2003 figures.
Sources: Hoover's; WetFeet analysis.

HOME CARE AND LONG-TERM CARE

If you enjoy working with people as they recuperate, you will want to consider career options in the emerging sector of home care, which is growing faster than the industry overall as the U.S. population ages.

Long-term and home care encompasses hospital-based skilled nursing facilities, intermediate care facilities, and custodial care facilities. Skilled nursing facilities offer high levels of medical and nursing care, including personal care and assistance for those with illnesses or impairments requiring lots of attention. Rehabilitative therapies and other prescribed medical services are also available. Typical stays at these facilities are only a few days or weeks. Intermediate-care facilities are designed for patients who are typically ambulatory with chronic illnesses or impairments that are less severe than those common to their counterparts in skilled nursing facilities. Licensed nurses or vocational nurses are always on hand, but services are directed toward long recovery periods typical of surgery or serious illnesses. Custodial care is designed for patients with the longest-term needs. They generally cost much less than other kinds of long-term care, since specialized medical attention is not generally necessary in this setting.

This sector also comprises hospices, which are organizations designed for the care of elders toward the end of their lives—generally the final 6 months. Provisions are made to manage symptoms so that their last days can be enjoyed in dignity and quality, surrounded by their loved ones. Hospices emphasize the quality of life, not "postponing death." Hospice care is typically available to the patient at home, with family members serving as the primary hands-on caregivers. Hospice care may also be available in hospitals, nursing homes, and private hospice facilities.

Advances in technology have done much to improve efficiency and reduce costs for both patients and long-term and home care staff. Today, long-term and home care nurses and aides can administer complex treatments—previously only available in hospitals or clinics—to the elderly and severely disabled, obviating the high costs and inconveniences traditionally associated with hospital stays. Almost all hospitals and HMOs now release patients before they become entirely self-sufficient, so these non-hospital care options have grown immensely in popularity in recent years.

Most jobs in this sector do not require much formal training, since they are supervised closely by RNs, NPs, or physicians. The downsides of work in this sector are notoriously low compensation and physically arduous work; not surprisingly, the level of worker satisfaction in this area lags that typical of more traditional forms of nursing. On the positive side, typical hours are generally quite flexible, and there is plenty of personal contact with clients in the unregimented and more peaceful settings of their own homes. Home care may offer a good fit for those just beginning to explore the health-care field or for those seeking part-time work.

Top Home Care and Long-Term Care Organizations

Organization	2004 Revenue ($M)	1-Year Growth Rate (%)	Employees
Kindred Healthcare	3,531	7.5	50,700
Manor Care*	3,414	6.5	59,400
Beverly Enterprises	1,989	−0.4	34,300
Mariner Health Care	1,715	−3.9	35,000
Select Medical Corp.	1,661	18.9	20,800
Life Care Centers of America**	1,600	9.6	30,000
Genesis HealthCare Corp.	1,530	n/a	35,000
Sunrise Senior Living	1,462	23.0	35,865
Extendicare	1,456	8.7	35,800
Apria Healthcare Group	1,451	5.1	11,178
NeighborCare	1,444	−45.5	6,100
Res-Care	1,009	5.0	30,000
Gentiva Health Services	846	3.9	14,550
Sun Healthcare Group	820	−1.7	n/a
The Evangelical Lutheran Good Samaritan Society	775	n/a	24,000
Visiting Nurse Service of New York	725	n/a	11,780
Five Star Quality Care	628	9.0	9,000
National HealthCare Corp.	522	23.4	12,000
Coram Healthcare Corp.**	477	9.9	3,000
American Retirement Corp.	448	21.6	9,245

*2005 figures; **2003 figures.
Sources: Hoover's; WetFeet analysis.

LABORATORIES AND RESEARCH

Collectively, laboratories represent one of the larger sectors of the health-care industry, and their role is critically important to the production of pharmaceuticals and therapeutics to effectively resolve persistent chronic diseases and other acute afflictions.

Clinical research labs are often engaged in performing clinical trials and related tasks for drugmakers' new drugs; these labs are contracted to do some or all of these tasks, depending on their clients' needs. These typically include the design, monitoring, and management of trials, the analysis of results, and other specialized duties that drug developers do not have the capacity to perform themselves. Clinical research labs facilitate, coordinate, and perform clinical trial studies on drugs in various stages of development. Examples of well known labs include Biovail and Quintiles. These organizations come in many shapes and sizes; some specialize in conducting early-stage clinical trials, while others perform studies in later stages.

Labs may also be involved in developing and conducting diagnostic tests and procedures like Pap smears, cholesterol checks, and HIV tests.

Although these organizations may not be well known by the masses, and their work is largely conducted behind the scenes, they do offer many job opportunities for highly trained health-care professionals (e.g., RNs, technicians) who work with patients, as well as for the clinical scientists who develop and administer the tests conducted by clinical research labs.

Top Clinical Research Labs

Organization	2004 Revenue ($M)	1-Year Growth Rate (%)	Employees
Quest Diagnostics*	5,504	7.4	38,600
Laboratory Corporation of America Holdings (LabCorp)*	3,378	7.9	23,500
Quintiles Transnational	2,146	4.9	16,986
Covance	1,056	8.4	6,700
PAREXEL International	659	6.4	4,875
AmeriPath	507	4.6	2,729
LabOne	468	35.3	3,100
Hooper Holmes	328	9.2	3,000
Severn Trent Laboratories	290*	n/a	n/a
Laboratory Sciences of Arizona	150*	n/a	1,000

*2005 figures.
Sources: Hoover's; WetFeet analysis.

Industry Trends

THE GROWING INFLUENCE OF HEALTH INSURANCE PROVIDERS

The biggest long-term trend in health care has been the growth of the managed-care approach to health services. Starting in the mid-1970s, in an effort to keep down sky-rocketing medical costs, insurance companies started taking a much more active role in the health-care industry.

Rather than simply continuing to pay for the treatments prescribed by doctors, who were often in private practice or employed by non-profit hospitals, insurance companies began forming groups, such as health maintenance organizations (HMOs) and pre-ferred provider organizations (PPOs), that combined the functions of hospitals and insurance companies.

While there are many different examples of these organizations—and each has its own set of complex rules—they share a common goal: to deliver medical services to their members at reduced rates by giving health-care providers incentives to keep costs down. Managed care in its various forms has swelled in popularity as employers have flocked to the cheaper plans, particularly HMOs.

Critics contend that managed-care plans lower the quality of health care by making doctors overly subject to cost constraints. Many charge that the cost savings achieved by managed-care plans come at the expense of patients' health. Others say that man-aged care is necessary to keep medical cost inflation under control, and to keep health care affordable and accessible to more people.

Both sides of the debate agree that, unless and until there's a political sea change in the United States and some kind of national health insurance program is enacted, the managed-care system has permanently changed the way medical services are delivered, and that patients and practitioners alike must adapt to the model.

TECHNOLOGY INNOVATIONS

Health care is a relative late-comer to high technology, but today, throughout the industry, organizations of all kinds are embracing advanced technology systems that do everything from managing patient records, storing X-ray images in digital format, and managing medical billing and payments to allowing patients to renew their prescriptions online and health-care practitioners to share information instantaneously despite being thousands of miles away from each other.

One insider notes that in situations where a patient needs immediate care late at night on the west coast, for instance, an Australian doctor many time zones away can step in.

In terms of U.S. job opportunities, the downside of this trend comes to light in the issue of outsourcing or off-shoring. Since IT-related services are far less costly in places like India and Asia, some health-care organizations have opted to send this kind of work overseas. This has become a hotly debated, contentious issue, but at this point there has been significantly less outsourcing of work overseas in health care, compared to other industries such as high technology.

RUNAWAY COSTS

Doctors and hospitals have been grappling with rising costs for a long time—and each year the problem seems to get worse. Malpractice insurance premiums, soaring prescription-drug prices, the increasing numbers of uninsured Americans, and rising salaries for nurses and ancillary support staff are all factors leading to ever-higher costs for caregivers. At the same time, revenues for doctors and hospitals keep falling, as insurers are doing everything in their power to lower payments for claims.

Meanwhile, insurers are not feeling the squeeze nearly as much as the caregivers. The reason: They make sure that revenues from premiums rise at a higher rate than claims payments.

Indeed, employers are facing double-digit percentage increases in health premium costs each year. The upshot: More and more of the cost of health insurance is being passed on to employees, meaning many people simply can no longer afford health-care coverage—considered a necessity (indeed, even a birthright, many argue) in any industrialized nation.

THE RISE OF NON-MAINSTREAM MEDICINE

Variously referred to as alternative or complementary medicine, older traditional techniques such as ayurveda, acupuncture, and others have been making a resurgence in this country over the past couple of decades. With established track records, these techniques are becoming increasingly recognized as legitimate by health-care authorities—and, perhaps more importantly, by insurers. For example, these days it's not uncommon for anesthesiologists running pain management clinics to refer certain patients for acupuncture treatment.

PREVENTION

There's a growing emphasis on preventative medicine in the United States. According to Dr David Sobel, regional director of patient education and health promotion at Kaiser Permanente in Northern California, through ongoing self-care and education, patients are becoming their own primary-care providers. Medical organizations of all kinds are becoming more vocal about getting their preventative-medicine messages out. Prevention programs in areas from smoking cessation to weight loss to stress management are popping up across the country. Incentive programs are becoming more prevalent in health-care plans. Indeed, in coming years, many health-care professionals' job descriptions will include offering education to patients—including those with no previous major health issues.

OBESITY

Obesity continues to represent one of the most persistent health threats in the United States. A host of other medical problems can be traced to obesity. Diseases linked to obesity include heart disease and diabetes. Today, in California (the nation's most populous state), an astonishing 53 percent of adults over 25 years old are overweight. More than 17 percent are obese or extremely overweight. A study prepared for the California Department of Health Services in 2005 by Chenoweth & Associates estimates that overweight and inactive Californians are responsible for $21.7 billion a year in medical bills, injuries, and lost productivity. As a people, Americans are gaining weight—and it's costing us when it comes time to pay society's health-care bill.

THE GROWING INFLUENCE OF THE PHARMACEUTICAL INDUSTRY

Drugmakers are facing criticism for in effect buying influence with state and federal government officials. For example, in early 2004, some U.S. senators called the National Institutes of Health to task for allowing its scientists to accept consulting compensation from pharmas and biotechs.

Similarly, a number of drug companies are coming under fire for driving the creation of new state drug guidelines used by state-run health facilities. The problem? These guidelines seemingly invariably direct state-employed physicians to prescribe expensive new drugs being sold under patent by the very companies who in effect wrote the state prescription guidelines.

Finally, some claim that one of the dirty secrets of the drug industry is that many expensive new drugs don't really work that well. According to these critics, most prescription drugs work only part of the time, and many can have potentially serious side effects. And in many cases, there are older, cheaper drugs available that could help many patients as well as newer, more expensive drugs, without the potential side effects of the newer drugs. Yet the drug companies, with their armies of salespeople, are able to create interest in new drugs among physicians (who don't have the time to really study the claims supporting the new drugs), and those physicians then prescribe those drugs in lieu of traditional alternatives.

CONSOLIDATION

As health-care costs rise and profit margins come under increasing pressure in almost all areas of health care, the industry has undergone extensive consolidation in an effort to leverage economies of scale and reduce risk. In 2004, for example, Anthem acquired WellPoint Health Networks (and renamed itself WellPoint) and UnitedHealth Group acquired Oxford Health Plans. In 2005, Coventry Health Care purchased First Health Group Corp. More recently, in 2006, medical equipment makers Guidant and Boston Scientific merged. Meanwhile, there have been all kinds of smaller M&A deals in the industry. The result of all this merger and acquisition activity is a continued decline in competition among health insurers—and higher premiums are one of the results.

LOWERING COSTS BY SHIFTING RESPONSIBILITIES

As health-care costs have risen, the industry has taken to shifting clinical and diagnostic responsibilities downward on the caregiving totem pole, to lower-cost classes of professionals. These days, for instance, many of the responsibilities that used to be handled only by MDs—such as prescribing drugs—are now handled by nurse practitioners, who are less expensive to employ than are doctors. This trend is apparent in many health-care specialty areas; in the eye-care field, for example, optometrists are now permitted to do some procedures than were once the exclusive province of ophthalmologists.

Picking and Choosing

How do you select the company or organization that is a perfect match for you? There are a number of factors to consider.

SIZE

Do you want to work for a big company, or a small one? Big organizations often mean a high degree of corporate politics and bureaucracy. On the flip side, they can offer a higher degree of job security, better compensation and benefits (such as training opportunities, tuition reimbursement, child care, and so on), and better (and more flexible) hours. Smaller employers are less likely to be able to afford to offer you such perks. Smaller organizations can be less bureaucratic—but if you work at the clinic of a very demanding MD, you may have to deal with long hours and high pressure.

Many health-care professionals choose to work for large organizations early in their careers, because that's where the jobs and the bulk of the training opportunities are, and then move to smaller organizations as they advance in their careers.

VARIETY AND FLEXIBILITY

For many, the greatest perk is variety and flexibility. Flex-time and unique job opportunities can be very attractive to some job candidates, such as those raising families or those seeking some adventures such as travel abroad. "Healthcare travelers," such as nurses, radiological technologists, physicians, therapists, and other professionals, are in great demand. Trained professionals can see the world as they earn. Currently, there is a strong need for such individuals in nursing.

LOCATION

Since health care workers are in demand in practically all parts of the country, you can generally work in the industry no matter where you live. If you've always wanted to live in the Southwest and would like to avoid the cold winters of your native New England, for example, making the move may be far easier for you than it would be for your cousin in consumer products.

The more specialized your career, of course, the more limited will be your options in terms of career location. As a researcher focusing on a highly specialized domain, for example, your options may be limited to just a few university clinical settings. If your area of specialization is one in which stem cells may be used, you may wisely consider moving to the San Francisco Bay Area, recently selected to be the headquarters of a multibillion-dollar statewide stem cell–based research program. Numerous research projects throughout the area are expected to create countless thousands of new jobs there in coming years.

OPPORTUNITIES TO WORK FOR THE BEST

There are lots of Type A personalities in health care, especially among doctors, and for these folks, it may be important to consider the status in the industry and among the public of potential employers. The Minnesota-based Mayo Foundation, for example, long rated among the best places to work in America, draws the best and the brightest, year in and year out. If your core competency matches their specialties and you get the opportunity, such a move may be a strategic one on your part, as having experience at a top-notch organization like this can help you write your ticket in terms of options later in your career.

LEVEL OF PATIENT CONTACT

This can be a big consideration when choosing your career and your employer. For example, if you get significant enjoyment out of working directly with patients, you will probably be happier working in a caregiving position than in a more administrative or research-oriented position. And the amount of patient contact you get can vary by organization as well as by career; for instance, in some hospitals an MD may have the opportunity for much greater interaction with patients than in other hospitals.

Those seeking to work with relatively little patient interaction might consider the emerging domain of IT in health care. This is a fast-evolving specialty that will offer increasing opportunities to well-trained medical personnel with an interest in technology.

The Firms

ADVENTIST HEALTH SYSTEM

111 North Orlando Avenue
Winter Park, FL 32789
Phone: 407-647-4400
Fax: 407-975-1469
www.ahss.org

Adventist Health System (AHS) was founded in Battle Creek, MI in 1866 by the Seventh Day Adventist Church. It operates some 38 hospitals, with a total of nearly 6,300 beds, in ten states. These hospitals serve some 3 million patients per year. AHS is one of the largest not-for-profit Protestant health care organizations in the United States.

AHS's home health care division, Sunbelt Home Health Care (SHHC), operates primarily in the southeastern United States, where it manages more than 20 home health and hospice agencies. SHHC operates 24 extended-care facilities with some 2,500 beds.

AHS's Florida Hospital system operates some 1,800 beds in central Florida, one of the company's top markets. Florida Hospital is the core facility, a tertiary care center with six campuses in the center of the state. Among the organization's diverse areas of specialization are cancer care, neuroscience, orthopedics, organ transplantation, "limb replantation," sports medicine, rehabilitation, and women's medicine.

In recent times, AHS has acquired three Denver-area hospitals and the Shawnee Mission Medical Center in that suburb of Kansas City. AHS hires health care and business professionals, and has operations in Michigan, Wisconsin, Illinois, Indiana, Kentucky, Tennessee, North Carolina, Georgia, Florida, Kansas, Colorado, and Texas. Careers are available in a wide range of health care fields and facility types, including behavioral health, cardiac care, eye care, MRI services, neurosurgery, obstetrics, orthopedics, pain medicine, radiology, rehab, and wellness.

Recent Milestones

2005   *U.S. News & World Report* ranks Florida Hospital 21st among U.S. hospitals in hormonal disorder treatment, 2th8 in neurology and neurosurgery, and 33rd in kidney disease.

      AHS's Jellico Community Hospital, Florida Hospital Flagler, and Shawnee Mission Medical Center rank among Solucient's "100 Top Hospitals for 2004," in a study of more than 3,000 hospitals.

      Fitch Ratings upgrades AHS-Sunbelt's $2.5 billion of outstanding debt to "A+" from "A."

2004   Florida Hospital Waterman receives a service excellence award from J.D. Power and Associates Distinguished Hospital Program, in recognition for providing an outstanding patient experience.

      AHS announces major expansion plans for its Florida Health system.

2003   Florida Hospital Fish Memorial receives certification for its Pulmonary and Cardiovascular Rehabilitation Program from the American Association of Cardiovascular and Pulmonary Rehabilitation.

      Emory-Adventist Hospital opens new Sinus Institute.

Key Financial Stats

2003 revenue: $10,123.1 million
1-year change: 20.0 percent

Personnel Highlights

Number of employees: 44,000
1-year change: 4.8 percent

AETNA

151 Farmington Avenue
Hartford, CT 06156
Phone: 860-273-0123
Phone (toll-free): 800-872-3862
Fax: 860-273-3971
www.aetna.com

Aetna's health insurance division offers one of the largest suites of combined services—everything from HMOs and PPOs to point-of- service (POS) plans and health savings accounts. One of the biggest health insurers around, Aetna sells life, disability, and long-term care insurance; dental, vision, and behavioral health plans; traditional indemnity coverage; and Medicare plans. It also offers pensions, annuities, and other retirement savings products.

Aetna has expanded via acquisition and other means a number of times in recent years. In 2003 it acquired pharmacy operations from Eckerd Health Services, and in 2004 it joined with Priority Healthcare to create the Aetna Specialty Pharmacy joint venture, a mail-order pharmacy business serving chronic disease sufferers. In 2005 Aetna brought its behavioral health offering in-house, purchasing the business, now called Aetna Behavioral Health, from Magellan Health Services. And today, at press time in early 2006, Aetna's in the process of acquiring ActiveHealth Management, a medical data analysis provider. Aetna increased its customer count by one million in 2005, a 6 percent increase. But Aetna needs to continue growing to keep up with its chief rivals, UnitedHealth Group and WellPoint—both of which serve about twice as many customers as does Aetna.

Examples of currently available positions range from nursing and information-technology-related positions, to sales and customer service, underwriting and actuarial—as well as audit-related areas.

Recent Milestones

2006   President Ron Williams succeeds Jack Rowe as Aetna's CEO.

2005   Announces its intent to purchase HMS Healthcare, a Denver-based regional health care network, for $390 million.

2004   In the domain of behavioral health care, Aetna announces plans to bring these services all in-house, terminating its relationship with Magellan Health Services.

As part of a move that will open its industry-leading discount dental network to more than 135 million U.S. citizens not already covered by dental insurance, the firm extends its innovative program entitled "Vital Savings by Aetna" to individuals. It offers patients admittance to nearly 53,000 available dental practice locations through Aetna Dental Access. The company claims this network saves its members an average of 28 percent on their bills.

Awarded a Medicare Chronic Care Improvement Program (CCIP) for metropolitan Chicago, accounting for some 20,000 such recipients in the greater Chicago area.

2003   Aetna InteliHealth's online interactive genetic testing guide is honored with a World Wide Web Health Award from the Health Information Resource Center.

Key Financial Stats

2004 revenue: $19,904.1 million
1-year change: 10.7 percent

Personnel Highlights

Number of employees: 26,700
1-year change: −3.3 percent

APRIA HEALTHCARE GROUP INC.

26220 Enterprise Court
Lake Forest, CA 92630
Phone: 949-639-2000
Phone (toll-free): 800-647-5404
Fax: 949-587-9363
www.apria.com

Apria offers integrative home-based health care services. Providing respiratory and infusion therapy as well as medical equipment such as hospital beds and wheel chairs, Apria is one of the largest firms in its sector in the country. Its respiratory therapy services treat patients for conditions including obstructive sleep apnea; chronic obstructive pulmonary diseases (COPD)—comprising diseases such as emphysema, asthma, bronchitis, various lung diseases including lung cancer; and pneumonia.

Apria also provides specialized equipment including oxygen concentrators, nebulizers, continuous positive airway pressure, respiratory assist devices, ventilators, and apnea monitors. Other kinds of home medical equipment it sells include wheelchairs and scooters, patient room equipment such as hospital beds and commodes, bathroom-based safety items such as safety rails for the bathtub, and transfer benches.

With nearly 34 regional infusion pharmacies, Apria is the third-largest home infusion provider in the United States. Its 1,500 trained respiratory, infusion nursing and clinical pharmacy specialists treat patients by communicating and coordinating care among the physician, payor, patient, and Apria's patient-support teams.

Apria operates through more than 500 branches serving some 1.3 million patients in all 50 states.

Positions currently open run the gamut from infusion services (with sales and pharmacy backgrounds desirable for certain jobs) to clinical services and distribution-related functions.

Recent Milestones

2006   Announces management reorganization aimed at maximizing sales growth.

2005   Signs with CIGNA to become that firm's preferred provider of home oxygen, respiratory equipment and services, home medical equipment, and enteral nutrition.

Pays the government $17.5 million to settle charges of improper Medicare billings.

2004   Apria buys some 30 businesses expressly to expand its respiratory therapy operations.

Key Financial Stats

2004 revenue: $1,451.4 million

1-year change: 5.1 percent

Personnel Highlights

Number of employees: 11,178

1-year change: 5.6 percent

ASCENSION HEALTH

4600 Edmundson Road
St. Louis, MO 63134
Phone: 314-733-8000
Fax: 314-733-8013
www.ascensionhealth.org

Among the largest nonprofit Catholic-based hospital systems in the nation, Ascension Health maintains a network of about 65 general acute-care hospitals and 12 long-term care, rehabilitation, and psychiatric hospitals. With its facilities primarily based in the southern, midwestern, and northeastern parts of the country, it prides itself in its mission of serving the poor and vulnerable in its role as a leading provider of "charity care" across the United States. It strives to adhere to its core values such as creatively grappling with difficult situations through "courageous innovation" and dedication to the community in which it serves its patients.

In order to save money, Ascension Health has sold a number of its hospitals that were no longer profitable. It continues to reorganize its facilities according to geographic regions, each headed by a vice president overseeing costs and management of its respective local region. In May of 2005, St. Joseph's Hospital in Augusta, Georgia, cut 100 personnel comprising nurses, technicians, and administration.

Jobs currently include more than 50 positions in nursing, more than 180 in primary care (physicians), as well as a few in administration.

Recent Milestones

2005   *U.S. News & World Report* ranks St. Vincent's in Jacksonville, Florida 37th among U.S. hospitals in heart surgery.

2004   The hospital was one of the first to spearhead the Institute of Healthcare Improvement 100,000 Lives Campaign. Intended to capture the attention of other hospitals nationwide, the campaign's goal is to institute changes that will prevent "avoidable deaths."

In recognition of its landmark efforts in creating conditions conducive to spirituality in the workplace, Ascension was bestowed with the international Spirit at Work Award held at an annual conference of the same name in Zurich, Switzerland.

2003   Launches its electronic medical records initiative. Information technology-based systems were developed to streamline information of patients' files throughout Ascension Health's facilities.

Merges with Catholic health-care provider Carondelet Health System.

Three Ascension Health ministries were included in Solucient's 100 Top Hospitals: Cardiovascular Benchmarks for Success.

Key Financial Stats

2003 revenue: $9,054.3 million

1-year change: 18.1 percent

Personnel Highlights

Number of employees: 105,000

1-year change: 0.0 percent.

BEVERLY ENTERPRISES, INC.

1000 Beverly Way
Fort Smith, AR 72919
Phone: 479-201-2000
Phone (toll-free): 877-823-8375
Fax: 479-201-1101
www.beverlycares.com

One of the nation's leading nursing home companies, Beverly Enterprises operates 351 nursing facilities, 18 assisted living centers, 52 hospice and home health locations, and 10 outpatient clinics in 23 states and in Washington, D.C. Beverly Enterprises offers a number of services through its subsidiaries: rehabilitation therapy services through AEGIS Therapies, nursing homes and assisted-living centers through Beverly Healthcare, and hospice and home-care services through AseraCare.

The firm has experienced shaky financial performance in recent years, due to changes in Medicare payment policy, and in response has shuttered more than 80 of its nursing homes as well as its MATRIX Rehabilitation subsidiary, which ran outpatient clinics specializing in occupational health and sports medicine. Beverly sold its Florida operations in 2002 due to high insurance-liability costs in the state. It also liquidated its Washington and Arizona operations and cut its California operations by a half due to patient liability costs.

Presently, the firm seeks to fill a handful of positions in nursing, specialist, and administrative positions.

Recent Milestones

2006   Completes merger with Fillmore Strategic Investors LLC.

2005   Affirmed its decision to sell the firm in an auction process. It had considered, but decided against following, one of its key investor's advice that it accept a takeover of the firm for $1.5 billion.

2004   Sold more than 80 nursing homes and its MATRIX Rehabilitation subsidiary, which ran outpatient therapy clinics specializing in occupational health and sports medicine.

        Finalized its purchase of Hospice USA, which operates facilities in 18 locations in Alabama, Mississippi, and Tennessee.

        One of 108 long-term care facilities in 36 states that earned the American Health Care Association (AHCA) and the National Center For Assisted Living's (NCAL) Quality Award for demonstrating its strong commitment to quality improvement.

Key Financial Stats

2004 revenue: $1,988.9 million

1-year change: −0.4 percent

Personnel Highlights

Number of employees: 34,300

1-year change: −5.5 percent

BLUE CROSS AND BLUE SHIELD ASSOCIATION

225 North Michigan Avenue
Chicago, IL 60601
Phone: 312-297-6000
Fax: 312-297-6609
www.bcbs.com

Blue Cross is an affiliation or "trade association" (in its own words) coordinating the activities of 38 independently operated regional chapters offering health-care coverage to some 93 million Americans, via indemnity insurance, HMOs, PPOs, point-of-service (POS) plans, and fee-for-service programs. These 40 entities collectively constitute the nation's oldest and largest family of health benefits companies. Association chapters also administer Medicare plans on behalf of the federal government. Blue Cross and Blue Shield member organizations insure one in every three Americans, and contract with more hospitals and doctors than any other insurer.

Blue Cross traces its roots back some 75 years, when the company's original ancestor began assuring hospital care to Texas teachers and providing physician care to lumber and mine workers in the Pacific Northwest.

Available positions at any time range from administrative, clerical, and information technology-related roles to professions requiring backgrounds in journalism or law. Montana's chapter is currently seeking actuarial analysts.

Recent Milestones

2005   Thirty one member organizations announce plans to charter a bank to handle customers' health savings accounts.

Consumer Reports ranks Blue Cross and Blue Shield member organizations in the top 10 spots in its PPO rankings.

Blue Cross and Blue Shield's Federal Employee Program grows its subscriber base for the 20th consecutive year.

2003   Announces worldwide medical coverage for expatriot Americans.

Key Financial Stats

2003 revenue: $182,700.0 million

1-year change: 12.2 percent

Personnel Highlights

Number of employees: 150,000

1-year change: 0 percent

EXTENDICARE INC.

Primary U.S. Office:
111 W. Michigan Street
Milwaukee, WI 53203
Phone: 414-908-8000
Phone (toll-free): 800-395-5000
Fax: 414-908-8059
www.extendicare.com

One of the largest operators of long-term care and assisted living facilities in North America, Extendicare is actually based in Canada but has a considerable presence in the United States; it serves 19 states, in addition to its considerable activity in Canada. Most of its activities are in the United States (which accounts for more than 70 percent of the firm's revenue). Of the firm's 78 facilities in Canada, 76 are nursing homes, one is a retirement home, and one is a chronic care unit. The firm's ParaMed subsidiary provides home health care services.

In all, Extendicare operates 442 locations with a collective capacity for some 34,500 residents. The firm provides specialty services in such medical areas as subacute care, rehabilitative therapy services, home health care, and assisted living.

Extendicare was licensed to build 11 new facilities in Ontario in 2001. It acquired Seven Leased Nursing Homes for $17.5 million in 2002.

Recent Milestones

2005   Extendicare plans to build eight assisted and independent living facilities adjacent to existing homes in the United States, thereby adding more than 300 new beds by 2006.

2005   Announces new president for Canadian operations, Paul Tuttle.

Acquires Assisted Living Concepts, comprising 177 assisted living facilities.

2004   Acquires four U.S. facilities totaling 321 beds.

Announces that Richard Bertrand is new CFO.

Key Financial Stats

2004 revenue: $1,455.8 million
1-year change: 8.7 percent

Personnel Highlights

Number of employees: 34,600
1-year change: not available.

HCA INC.

1 Park Plaza
Nashville, TN 37203
Phone: 615-344-9551
Fax: 615-344-2266
www.hcahealthcare.com

HCA was founded in 1968 by Dr. Thomas Frist, Sr., Dr. Thomas Frist, Jr., and Jack Massey, in Nashville. Today the company operates some 190 hospitals and 91 outpatient surgery centers, representing 44,000 beds and 22,000 ambulatory surgery centers, in 23 states, England, and Switzerland.

The firm is notorious for the way its activities have helped alter the U.S. health-care landscape. One of the first hospital management companies, HCA, which operated 11 hospitals when it sold its IPO in 1969, grew to 349 hospitals by 1981 and 463 hospitals by 1987. In that year, HCA spun off the 104-hospital HealthTrust. In 1994, HCA merged with Columbia, which had acquired the former Humana in the previous year. The merged company then acquired a series of other health care businesses, growing to more than 350 hospitals, 145 outpatient surgery centers, and 550 home care agencies. HCA refocused in 1999, reducing in size to 190 hospitals, when it spun off two hospital companies, Triad and LifePoint. The 2003 purchase of the 12-hospital Health Midwest system marked HCA's return to more acquisitive ways.

In recent years, emergency room (ER) visits by and inpatient admissions of uninsured patients have continued to rise, meaning that HCA has an increasing amount of bad debt. Reacting to a rise in debt and public criticism of efforts to collect cash from uninsured patients, HCA in late 2003 instituted a sliding scale for many uninsured patients.

Recent Milestones

2006   Closes sale of five hospitals to LifePoint Hospitals.

2005   Completes sale of five hospitals in Tennessee, Oklahoma, Washington, and Louisiana to Capella Healthcare.

A series of class action lawsuits alleging financial reporting misconduct are filed against HCA.

Republican Senator Bill Frist, a member of the family that founded HCA, comes under fire for selling shares in the company just prior to a public profit warning announcement, which sent HCA share prices tumbling.

SEC begins investigating insider sales of HCA shares.

Acquires Tennessee Christian Medical Centers' operations from Adventist Health System.

2003   Pays nearly $650 million to settle U.S. Department of Justice charges relating to HCA's cost reports and physician relations.

HCA acquires a 12-hospital system in Kansas City. The former Health Midwest hospitals become HCA's new Midwest Division.

HCA finishes paying out some 2 billion dollars in settlements for Medicare fraud and other claims over the previous 5 years.

2002   Jack Bovender becomes HCA's chairman of the board.

Key Financial Stats

2004 revenue: $23,502.0 million
1-year change: 7.8 percent

Personnel Highlights

Number of employees: 191,400
1-year change: 1.8 percent

HEALTHSOUTH CORPORATION

1 HealthSouth Parkway
Birmingham, AL 35243
Phone: 205-967-7116
Phone (toll-free): 888-476-8849
Fax: 205-969-6889
www.healthsouth.com

With facilities in the United States, Australia, Puerto Rico, and the United Kingdom, HealthSouth, a provider of diagnostic imaging, rehabilitative health care, and outpatient surgery services, is one of the biggest health-care companies around. But it hasn't been all wine and roses for the company in recent times; HealthSouth was nearly run into the ground by founder and former CEO, Richard Scrushy, who was ousted from the chief executive position in 2003, after extensive financial fraud was revealed at the company.

Today HealthSouth is focused on a cost-conscious strategy, while it tries to change its corporate culture from a CEO-centered one to one that pays more attention to employees.

HealthSouth contracts with leading insurers, managed care plans, and big-name firms such as Delta Air Lines, Goodyear Tire & Rubber, and Winn-Dixie Stores, in addition to a host of professional sports associations, universities, and high schools, but most of its revenue comes from government-funded health plans, particularly Medicare.

The firm was co-founded by Scrushy and a handful of co-workers, with the intention of running rehabilitation centers that are less like hospitals and more like upscale health clubs. Today it operates nearly 100 inpatient rehabilitation facilities, 765 outpatient rehab facilities, 177 ambulatory surgery centers and 3 surgical hospitals, and 96 diagnostic centers

Recent Milestones

2006 The fact that former CEO Richard Scrushy paid journalists to write positive stories during his fraud trial becomes public.

   Scrushy is ordered to repay company $48 million in company performance-related bonuses he fraudulently received while CEO.

2005 Scrushy is cleared of criminal charges in lawsuit over accounting fraud at HealthSouth.

   Company settles with SEC over accounting fraud, for $100 million.

2003 The SEC initiates an investigation of HealthSouth's accounting practices, leading to the firing of chairman and CEO Richard Scrushy, removal of the company's auditor, and delisting of the company's stock by the NYSE.

Key Financial Stats

2004 revenue: $3,753.8 million

1-year change: −5 percent

Personnel Highlights

Number of employees: 40,000

1-year change: 0 percent

KAISER PERMANENTE

1 Kaiser Plaza, Suite 2600
Oakland, CA 94612
Phone: 510-271-5800
Fax: 510-267-7524
www.kaiserpermanente.org

Founded in 1945, Kaiser Permanente is a nonprofit health plan—the largest HMO in the United States. California is by far Kaiser's biggest source of revenue; of the company's 8.2 million enrolled members, 6.2 million of them are in that state. Kaiser Permanente also has a presence in Colorado, Georgia, Hawaii, Maryland, Ohio, Oregon, Virginia, Washington, and Washington, D.C.

Kaiser traces its roots back to industrial health-care programs for construction, shipyard, and steel-mill workers in the 1930s and 1940s. Today some 11,000 physicians practice with Kaiser, and the company operates 30 hospitals as well as more than 500 other locations.

Kaiser Permanente actually owns hospitals only in California, Hawaii, and Oregon; it provides services to its members in the other areas it operates through contracts with health-care facilities. The company maintains an alliance with Group Health Cooperative—in effect extending its network into the Pacific Northwest.

The company is currently doling out a fair amount of money in California, spending more than $1.2 billion to build four new hospitals and elevating its facilities to full compliance with earthquake safety codes.

Kaiser is active in research; at any given time, there are around 2,000 studies being conducted involving Kaiser Permanente clinicians and researchers.

Recent Milestones

2005   Begins offering members the ability to e-mail questions to Kaiser doctors.

Agrees to new 5-year contract with the Coalition of Kaiser Permanente Unions, covering 82,000 employees.

Receives more three-star or excellent ratings than any other surveyed health plan in the state in California's 2005 Quality of Care Report Card.

2004   Launches new website providing free public health-care information.

Begins offering health savings accounts.

2003   Kaiser announces plans to spend some $3 billion through 2013 on administrative technology.

Launches KP Connect, its electronic medical records system, one that some say will revolutionize the way health care is delivered—not to mention save Kaiser a bundle of money in administrative costs.

Key Financial Stats

2003 revenue: $25,300.0 million
1-year change: 12.4 percent

Personnel Highlights

Number of employees: 147,000
1-year change: 7.7 percent

KINDRED HEALTHCARE, INC.

680 S. 4th Street
Louisville, KY 40202
Phone: 502-596-7300
Fax: 502-596-4170
www.kindredhealthcare.com

Kindred operates 73 hospitals (5,603 licensed beds) in 24 states; 245 nursing centers (31,323 licensed beds) in 28 states; an institutional pharmacy business with 39 pharmacies in 23 states; a pharmacy management business servicing the company's hospitals; and a contract rehabilitation services business.

Franklin Mutual Advisers (a division of Franklin-Templeton, the mutual fund giant) owns about a quarter of the company. Medicare and Medicaid reimbursements make up more than 70 percent of Kindred's revenue; historically it has collected at least half its revenue from government plans.

Changes in Medicare and Medicaid payment processes and charges of Medicare fraud hurt the company in the late 1990s, and it operated in bankruptcy from 1999 to 2001.

Recent Milestones

2005   Opens hospital in Ocala, FL, and announces plans to open new Cleveland hospital in 2006.

Purchases four long-term acute-care hospitals from Health Care REIT, Inc.

Acquires RXPERTS, a pharmacy company.

Acquires the long-term acute care hospital, skilled nursing facility, and assisted living facility assets of Commonwealth Community Holdings LLC.

Announces plans to open new hospitals in Pennsylvania and Arizona.

Acquires Pharmacy Partners, Inc., and Skilled Care Pharmacy.

2004   Begins operating its contract rehabilitation business as a separate division.

2003   Sells all of its Texas and Florida nursing center operations.

Key Financial Stats

2004 revenue: $3,531.2 million

1-year change: 7.5 percent

Personnel Highlights

Number of employees: 50,700

1-year change: 0 percent

LABORATORY CORPORATION OF AMERICA HOLDINGS (LABCORP)

358 S. Main Street
Burlington, NC 27215
Phone: 336-229-1127
Phone (toll-free): 800-334-5261
Fax: 336-436-1205
www.labcorp.com

One of the world's largest clinical research laboratories, Laboratory Corporation of America Holdings conducts testing for physicians, government agencies, managed care organizations, hospitals, clinical labs, and pharmaceutical companies. Its range of testing functions run the gamut from routine testing (such as blood chemistry analyses, urinalyses, blood cell counts, Pap tests, HIV tests, microbiology cultures and procedures, and alcohol and other substance-abuse tests) to specialty testing services (including allergy testing; clinical trials testing; oncology testing in which it diagnoses and monitors certain cancers, and predicts the outcome of certain treatments; HIV genotyping and phenotyping; diagnostic genetics that include cytogenetic, molecular cytogenetic, biochemical, and molecular genetic tests; and urine and blood testing services for the detection of drug and alcohol abuse). LabCorp also provides anatomic pathology testing services in uropathology, dermatopathology, GI pathology, and hematopathology areas.

LabCorp operates 35 major labs, plus about 1,300 patient service sites nationally. It offers over 4,400 clinical tests, and performs diagnostic procedures on some 360,000 specimens per day.

To bolster its presence in North America, it bought Dynacare in 2002, introducing some 445 facilities to its roster as it did so. It then picked up DIANON Systems in early 2003 and US Pathology Labs in 2005. These acquisitions have fortified its cancer diagnostic operations.

The firm recently agreed to acquire specialty reference testing firm Esoterix, which operates nine labs in the United States and Europe.

Recent Milestones

2006   *Forbes* ranks Laboratory Corporation of America Holdings as one of the best big U.S. companies.

2005   Purchases US Pathology Labs to develop its cancer diagnostic operations, which the firm views as one of its key markets.

    ViroMed introduces avian flu test.

    Names David King as COO.

    Acquires testing company Esoterix, Inc.

2004   Standard & Poor's (S&P) added the company to the S&P 500 Index Laboratory Corporation of America® Holdings (NYSE: LH).

    Signs deal to provide all Swedish medical center laboratory services.

2003   Acquires Northern California operations of Quest Diagnostics.

    Acquires DIANON Systems in early 2003, through which the company has collaborated with firms such as Myriad Genetics and Celera Diagnostics to offer gene-based cancer testing.

Key Financial Stats

2005 revenue: $3,327.6 million
1-year change: 7.9 percent

Personnel Highlights

Number of employees (2004): 23,500
1-year change: 2.2 percent

MANOR CARE, INC.

333 N. Summit Street
Toledo, OH 43604
Phone: 419-252-5500
Fax: 419-252-5596
www.hcr-manorcare.com

Through its operating group HCR Manor Care, Manor Care is one of the nation's leading providers of short-term post-acute medical care and long-term skilled nursing care. It operates more than 275 skilled nursing facilities, 65 assisted-living facilities, hospice services, home health care services, and nearly 90 outpatient therapy clinics which provide rehab services at work sites, schools, assisted living facilities, homes, hospitals, and so on. The company is making a big push to attract Alzheimer's patients, since that market is sure to grow as the Baby Boomers age. The company's facilities operate under the HeartLand, Manor Care, Arden Courts, and Springhouse brands. Its operations are focused in the Midwest, the Mid-Atlantic states, Florida, and Texas.

The company has been hurt in recent times by bad debt, primarily from Medicare patients, despite serving a smaller amount of patients (by number of Medicare patients to overall patient count) than many competitors. The company traces its history back to the 1940s, when the Wolfe family purchased an Ohio lumber company that would later become Health Care and Retirement Company of America (HCR). The company has grown via acquisition over the years, taking on Manor Care's name in 1998.

The Manor Care portion of the company traces its roots back to a Maryland nursing home built in 1959. Manor Care owned lodging brands like Econo Lodge, Quality Inn, and Clarion Hotels and Resorts until it spun them off in the mid-1990s.

Recent Milestones

2006   CFO Geoffrey Myers announces he's retiring after 39 years with Manor Care and predecessor companies.

       Ranked among "America's Best Big Companies" by *Forbes*.

2004   Divests 21 skilled nursing and assisted living facilities.

Key Financial Stats

2005 revenue: $3,414.3 million

1-year change: 6.5 percent

Personnel Highlights

Number of employees (2004): 59,400

1-year change: –2.6 percent

MAYO FOUNDATION FOR MEDICAL EDUCATION AND RESEARCH

200 1st Street S.W.
Rochester, MN 55905
Phone: 507-284-2511
Fax: 507-284-0161
www.mayo.edu

The Mayo Foundation found its genesis in Minnesota in 1863 when two brothers—both doctors—envisioned a new way of practicing medicine through a unique blending of research, clinical teamwork, and education. Today, Mayo has grown to three clinics and four hospitals in Minnesota, Arizona, and Florida—plus a Minnesota retirement community and a network of clinics and hospitals in 62 communities in Minnesota, Wisconsin, and Iowa. Now, as always, the organization focuses on providing the best care possible for all its patients.

The foundation also provides medical education at the Mayo Medical School, Mayo Graduate School of Medicine, and Mayo School of Health-Related Sciences, as well as by conducting its own biomedical research. Since the foundation's charter forbids it to raise its prices, it has established a unique system of its own income-generating companies. In order to account for growing health care costs, it generates revenues through its publications, medical technologies, and investments in selected medical-based start-up companies. The foundation treats more than 500,000 patients a year.

Recent Milestones

2005   *US News & World Report* ranks the Mayo Clinic first among U.S. hospitals in treating digestive orders, hormonal disorders, neurology and neurosurgery, and orthopedics; second in gynecology, heart and heart surgery, respiratory disorders, and rheumatology; third in kidney disease and urology; fourth in rehabilitation; fifth in cancer and ear, nose, and throat; seventh in geriatrics; 12th in psychiatry; 13th in ophthalmology; and 21st in pediatrics. The magazine also ranks Mayo Clinic Arizona (in Phoenix, AZ) 26th in respiratory disorders.

Ranked 26th of the "100 Best Companies to Work For" by *Fortune*.

2004   Chosen by the National Cancer Institute (NCI) to participate in a new initiative to test the effectiveness of experimental medications and nutritional compounds for prevention of cancer. It is one of six such selected research centers in the United States.

2003   Two generous families donate a total of $10 million to Mayo Clinic to advance the progress of medical research in Alzheimer's disease—the largest contributions it has received at one time for Alzheimer's disease research.

Key Financial Stats

2004 revenue: $3.2 million

1-yr. change: 5.9 percent

Personnel Highlights

Number of employees (2003): 42,620

1-year change: 2.6 percent

QUEST DIAGNOSTICS INCORPORATED

1290 Wall Street West
Lyndhurst, NJ 07071
Phone: 201-393-5000
Phone (toll-free): 800-222-0446
Fax: 201-462-4715
www.questdiagnostics.com

Quest is one of the world's foremost clinical research labs. Quest Diagnostics conducts close to 140 million tests annually—from the mundane, such as cholesterol checks, Pap smears, HIV screenings, and alcohol tests, to the elaborate, such as genetic screening and toxicology.

The company serves a host of different kinds of clients. They range from doctors and hospitals to HMOs, government agencies, and prisons to client companies—even other labs themselves. The firm maintains in excess of 1,900 patient service centers where samples are collected, in conjunction with some 30 primary labs and about 140 rapid response labs across the United States and in Mexico and the UK.

Quest is currently targeting genetic and predictive testing as areas of particular growth; increasingly, doctors and patients have been seeking to identify potential issues well in advance in order to lower overall health care costs.

About a fifth of Quest is owned by GlaxoSmithKline, the pharmaceutical giant; Quest conducts half of all clinical trials for GlaxoSmithKline.

Recent Milestones

2005   The firm's MedPlus healthcare information technology subsidiary is recognized in "Year-End Best in KLAS Awards" as the number-one document management and imaging (DMI) vendor in 2004: The award was conferred upon Quest for its ChartMaxx enterprise-wide electronic record solution for hospitals.

2004   Consummates agreements with RxHub, Medco Health Solutions and Express Scripts to gain online access to their pharmacy benefit services and information. Quest Diagnostics is the only CLA with access to RxHub. RxHub is a joint venture formed in 2001 by Medco, AdvancePCS (acquired by Caremark Rx), and Express Scripts—three of the leading pharmacy benefit managers in the United States.

In the prestigious *InformationWeek* 500 ranking, honored as one of the "Top 100 Innovators" in the United States.

2003   Acquires Unilab.

Key Financial Stats

2005 revenue: $5,503.7 million

1-year change 7.4 percent

Personnel Highlights

Number of employees (2004): 38,600

1-year change: 3.8 percent

QUINTILES TRANSNATIONAL CORP.

P.O. Box 13979
Research Triangle Park, NC 27709
Phone: 919-998-2000
Fax: 919-998-2094
www.quintiles.com

Quintiles helps drug and medical-device companies with product development, marketing, and sales. It is one of the world's largest clinical research organizations, focused on advancing all levels of pharmaceutical and clinical research. Quintiles handles early stage development and laboratory services, clinical development services, and research services. According to the company, "Of the world's top 30 best-selling drugs, Quintiles' teams helped develop or commercialize every one."

Quintiles' PharmaBio Development business assists smaller companies in bringing products to market by exchanging its R&D expertise for royalties on products it helps bring to market.

In a joint venture with McKesson Corporation, in 2002 Quintiles formed Verispan, L.L.C., which provides health-care informatics products.

Headquartered in Research Triangle Park, Quintiles has locations in more than 10 U.S. states, as well as in Canada, Argentina, Brazil, Chile, Mexico, Peru, India, South Africa, Australia, China, Malaysia, New Zealand, the Philippines, Singapore, Taiwan, Thailand, and across Europe.

Recent Milestones

2005   Roche signs a 3-year clinical-management services contract with Quintiles.

Announces joint venture to commercialize products in the Asia-Pacific region.

2004   Enters an agreement with Pacific Biometrics, Inc., a provider of specialty central laboratory services, to co-promote and co-market its central laboratory services.

2003   The firm is taken private and merged with Pharma Services Acquisition Corp. (Merger Sub), a subsidiary of Pharma Services Holding, Inc. by Chairman Dennis Gillings.

Key Financial Stats

2004 revenue: $2,146.3 million

1-year change: 4.9 percent

Personnel Highlights

Number of employees: 16,986

1-year change: 6.2 percent

TENET HEALTHCARE CORPORATION

13737 Noel Road
Dallas, TX 75240
Phone: 469-893-2200
Fax: 469-893-8600
www.tenethealth.com

Tenet is one of the big daddies of the hospital business. It owns or operates 114 acute care hospitals and related businesses with nearly 28,000 beds in 16 states. Founded in 1969 by three attorneys as National Medical Enterprises (NME), the company quickly went public and subsequently acquired many new hospitals and health-care facilities.

In 1992, NME was raided by federal agents on suspicion of insurance fraud, based on allegations by insurance companies. So far, the company has paid out more than $370 million to settle various charges, including the alleged abuse of psychiatric patients.

NME changed its name to Tenet in 1995 to reflect its firm tenets and values. The new name didn't necessarily mean a new way of doing business, however; Tenet has settled charges that doctors at one of its hospitals conducted unnecessary cardiac operations; faced charges that it overbilled Medicare; settled class-action charges claiming the company lied about its financial condition; and faced a probe of deaths at one of its New Orleans hospitals following Hurricane Katrina. Trouble at Tenet has resulted in the departure during the following several years of some 40 percent of the executives who'd been working at the company in 2002, and in 2006 the company announced it would restate earnings from 2000 to 2003.

As part of an ongoing effort to ameliorate its public image, Tenet has initiated a discount program for uninsured patients that would charge prices similar to those paid by their managed care counterparts.

Recent Milestones

2005   Moves its headquarters from Santa Barbara, California, to Dallas.

Agrees to settlement in which Health Net pays $28.5 million to settle its debt to Tenet California.

2004   Sells off eleven home-health agencies and two home hospices as part of its strategy directed toward reducing its holdings. Nearly 30 hospitals are part of the sale, including 19 in California as well as eight others in Louisiana and Massachusetts.

2003   Announces it will collaborate on two major industry initiatives designed to advance quality care and improve patient safety at the nation's hospitals. The American Hospital Association, the Association of American Medical Colleges, and the Federation of American Hospitals are some of the participants.

Key Financial Stats

2004 revenue: $9,919.0 million

1-year. change: –24.9 percent

Personnel Highlights

Number of employees: 91,633

1-year change: –16.5 percent

UNIVERSAL HEALTH SERVICES, INC.

Universal Corporate Center
367 S. Gulph Rd.
King of Prussia, PA 19406
Phone: 610-768-3300
Fax: 610-768-3336
www.uhsinc.com

UHS was founded in 1978 by Alan B. Miller. Today it's the fourth-largest hospital company in the United States, with 44 acute-care hospitals and 49 behavioral-health centers in the United States, France, and Puerto Rico. It also operates ambulatory surgery and radiation oncology centers.

The company's strategy is to build or purchase health-care operations in fast-growing markets. It's been particularly aggressive in recent years in building out its behavior and mental-health operations. For example, it recently purchased Keystone Youth Services, a network of youth treatment centers, as well as the Center for Change, an eating-disorder facility in Utah, and the Wyoming Behavioral Institute, a behavioral-health treatment center.

Several Universal hospitals were affected by Hurricane Katrina; patients and staff at its River Oaks Hospital in New Orleans were transplanted to a Universal hospital in Tennessee.

UHS operates in several northeastern states, the southern and southeastern United States., and in several western states and Alaska—in all, in 24 states plus Washington, D.C., and Puerto Rico.

Recent Milestones

2005   Named by *Forbes* as one of the "Best Big Companies in the U.S."

Sells Medi-Partenaires, one of the largest private hospital companies in France.

Acquires Keystone Youth Services, comprising 40 outpatient, inpatient, and residential treatment facilities.

Sells two hospitals in Puerto Rico.

2004   Named by *Computerworld* as one of the "100 Best Places to Work in IT."

2003   Announces acquisition of Lakeland Medical Center in New Orleans.

Ranks as the top health-care provider investment among Fortune 1000 companies during the previous 10 years.

Key Financial Stats

2004 revenue: $3,938.3 million

1-year change: 8.1 percent

Personnel Highlights

Number of employees: 37,000

1-year change: 5.7 percent

WELLPOINT, INC.

120 Monument Circle
Indianapolis, IN 46204
Phone: 317-488-6000
Fax: 317-488-6028
www.wellpoint.com

Among the largest health insurance companies in the United States, WellPoint (formerly known as Anthem) is the Blue Cross licensee for California, and the Blue Cross and Blue Shield licensee for Colorado, Connecticut, Georgia, Indiana, Kentucky, Maine, Missouri, Nevada, New Hampshire, Ohio, Virginia, and Wisconsin. The company serves some 34 million members nationwide, through a variety of PPOs, HMOs, various hybrid and specialty network-based dental and health-care services, as well as flexible spending accounts and COBRA administration

The company was created by the 2004 merger of Anthem (which traces its roots back to Blue Cross and Blue Shield of Indiana) and WellPoint Health Networks (which traces its roots back to Blue Cross of California). In 2005 WellPoint merged with WellChoice, making New York the 14th state in which WellPoint is a Blue Cross/Blue Shield licensee.

Recent Milestones

2005   Acquires Lumenos, a provider of health savings accounts and health reimbursement accounts.

Ranks 97th on the 2005 Fortune 500 list.

Merges with WellChoice, expanding into New York in the process.

2004   Company is formed through the merger of Anthem and WellPoint Health Networks.

2003   WellPoint acquires Golden West Dental and Vision

WellPoint acquires Cobalt Corp., which runs Blue Cross and Blue Shield United of Wisconsin.

Key Financial Stats

2005 revenue: $45,136.0 million

1-year change: 116.8 percent

Personnel Highlights

Number of employees (2004): 38,000

1-year change: 88.8 percent

On the Job

The Big Picture

Key Jobs

Real People Profiles

The Big Picture

As discussed earlier, because the Baby Boom generation is reaching retirement age these days—and because, as America's most well-off generation, the Baby Boomers have plenty of money to spend on health care as they get older and more frail—there are going to be an increasing number of career opportunities in the health-care sector for the next decade and possibly beyond.

RNs, pharmacists, medical technicians, and people in many other health-care professions are currently in very high demand and will continue to be in demand in the decade ahead. Why? The Baby Boomer population is maturing into retirement, the elderly population in the United States is growing, and health-care spending is being cut wherever possible—which means that today, whenever a nurse can do something a doctor used to be responsible for, that's exactly what's going to happen. Employers are looking to attract people to these in-demand professions by offering signing bonuses, tuition reimbursement or loan repayment, flexible scheduling, and incentives for voluntary overtime shifts.

Opportunities will also grow at a healthy clip for other health-care functions, from doctor, PA, and optometrist to occupational therapist, audiologist, and physical therapist to home-health aide, medical record technologist, medical transcriptionist, and speech pathologist.

Many health-care organizations offer jobs in management in addition to medicine. Technical and administrative support positions are in high demand as the industry evolves in an intensely competitive market. Health-care IT is a steadily growing sector; although the industry has been a late adopter of IT, it is catching up now. There will be lots of opportunity in this area for the tech-savvy.

HOSPITALS

Hospitals are the largest employers in the industry. This is where some 60 percent of nurses work, for example. Huge health-care networks such as Kaiser and Tenet are always seeking doctors, nurses, administrators, medical technicians, therapists, and ancillary support staff. The range of positions commonly found in hospitals run the gamut from orderly to physician. As is true at most other kinds of health-care institutions, nurses comprise the largest single group of professionals at hospitals—and, as is true in most other kinds of health-care institutions, there's a nursing shortage in the hospital sector, meaning lots of opportunities—and upward pressure on wages—for these caregiving professionals. And many other hospital careers will see notable growth in coming years.

That's not to say that hospital careers are not subject to risks. As the trend toward reducing costs continues, expect to see fairly regular hospital closures and lots of merger and acquisition activity in the sector. Also expect more and more frequent battles between hospital management and labor. The reason: Because of pressures from investors to cut costs, nurses and many other hospital professionals are being asked to do more and more as part of their jobs, at the same time as they're being asked to shoulder more and more of the costs of their benefits.

SPECIALTY PROVIDERS

With the continued rise in costs of hospital services, there has been a trend toward outsourcing more kinds of services traditionally administered only in the hospital environment, to outpatient clinics and—more and more—directly to the patient's home. Organizations in this sector include nursing homes, kidney dialysis centers, physical and occupational therapy clinics, addiction therapy centers, blood banks, fertility clinics, chemotherapy providers, MRI clinics, and so on. As is true elsewhere in health care, the biggest single job category among specialty providers is nursing, but there will be job growth for everyone from doctors to medical technicians to business and administrative types in this sector in coming years.

HOME CARE AND LONG-TERM CARE

The geriatric home-based care sector is expected to explode as Baby Boomers begin to enter old age. One insider notes that from 2010 and until 2030, 10,000 people will turn 65 every day. As a result, there's a growing need for nursing, MD, and other graduates with expertise is gerontology and other areas significant to the elderly, such as orthopedics and rheumatology.

The number of jobs for home-care aides is expected to grow at an exceptionally high rate in coming years. Aides assist patients with simple daily functions such as eating, personal hygiene, and others.

A downside of this sector for job seekers is that salaries are typically not as high in home care and long-term care as they are in hospitals and other clinical settings. But there are other advantages to consider. For one thing, this sector offers a prevalence of flex- and part-time work plans, making it a good option for students who are looking to learn on the job as well as older workers with family or other responsibilities.

RESEARCH ORGANIZATIONS

Labs can be found in many settings—at hospitals (labs are common in hospitals that are part of university medical centers) as well as in separate organizations specializing in clinical trials studies for pharmaceuticals and/or clinicial testing. Whether you are a recent college graduate with a science background or someone with nursing experience, you can find opportunities in this sector.

Other jobs to be had in this sector include medical liaison and principal investigator. Medical liaisons, who generally have Ph.D.s in a bio-medical discipline, work closely with doctors and researchers on drug discovery-based projects. Principal investigators (PIs) are responsible for obtaining grants and establishing niches in particular specialties. Some eventually move into other areas—such as marketing and PR—within these organizations.

HMOS/PPOS

With a nursing degree in hand, candidates can expect to land a wide range of jobs in nursing services in HMOs and PPOs. Advice nurses are in demand at various insurance provider organizations; for example, Blue Cross's Medcall offers answers to medical answers over the phone at all hours of the day, every day of the week in non-emergency situations. Nurses who perform these services are typically required to have about 5 years' experience under their belts already. Nurses are involved in performing cost-benefit analyses as well as marketing services for such organizations.

These organizations also employ quite a few IT types to implement and manage their advanced technology systems. There are also a lot of business jobs in this sector.

Key Jobs

PHYSICIANS

MDs and DOs

Doctors belong to a complex and challenging profession, but have a simple goal: to treat and heal people who are suffering from injury or disease. As part of their practice, doctors examine patients, evaluate medical histories, perform and interpret medical tests, make medical diagnoses, and prescribe and administer treatments that may include surgery, drugs, physical therapies, or other types of treatment.

Many of these activities are done in conjunction with other professionals such as nurses and clinical laboratory technologists, but ultimately the doctor is responsible for diagnosing the patient and deciding upon a course of treatment.

Increasingly, doctors are also involved in keeping patients healthy through preventative care, which often includes counseling patients about diet, exercise, and stress reduction. Preventative medicine has become more popular in recent years as managed care emphasizes cost controls and the prevention of illnesses that may be expensive to treat.

There are two types of physician: MDs (doctors of medicine, also known as allopathic physicians) and DOs (doctors of osteopathic medicine). Both can perform the full range of medical services for patients, including surgery and drug therapy. The main difference is that DOs are more focused on the proper functioning of the body's musculoskeletal system and place more emphasis on preventative medicine. Both MDs and DOs can be found in general medical practices or various specializations.

General Practitioners

General or family practitioners have always been common in the medical field, but are more prevalent than ever today due to the dominance of managed care. Managed-care systems emphasize the role of the primary-care physician: the patient's regular doctor, who typically must authorize referrals to specialists or nonemergency admissions to the hospital.

Primary-care physicians generally specialize in internal medicine, family medicine, pediatrics, or geriatrics. Because general practitioners have become increasingly responsible for their patients, they must be able to recognize a wider range of conditions, to recommend appropriate treatments, and to refer patients to specialists.

Salary ranges for primary-care physicians:

- Internal medicine: $125,000 to $180,000

- Family practice: $125,000 to $175,000

- Pediatrics: $115,000 to $170,000

- Geriatrics: $120,000 to $190,000

SPECIALISTS

Medical specialists focus on a specific area of the body, a particular type of illness or condition, or a certain procedure.

Body-related specialties include cardiopulmonary medicine (heart and lungs), gynecology (female reproductive system), dermatology (skin), immunology (immune system), endocrinology (endocrine glands), gastroenterology (digestive organs), hematology (blood, spleen, and lymph glands), hepatology (liver and biliary tract), neurology (brain, spinal cord, and nervous system), ophthalmology (eye), otolaryngology (ear, respiratory, and upper alimentary systems), rheumatology (joints, muscles, bones, and tendons), and urology (adrenal gland and genitourinary system).

Condition-related specialists focus on allergy (reactions to irritating agents), oncology (cancer and other benign or malignant tumors), toxicology (poisoning cases), and obstetrics (pregnancy, labor, and delivery).

Procedure-related specialties include anesthesiology (managing patients' pain and consciousness during and after operations and other procedures), radiology (using radiation to diagnose and treat patients), and surgery (using invasive operative techniques to diagnose and treat patients). Many specialties have subspecialties—for instance, a doctor might specialize in head and neck surgery, radiation oncology (use of radiation to treat cancer), or pediatric cardiovascular surgery.

Salary ranges for various specialties:

- Anesthesiologist: $206,000 to $295,000

- Cardiologist: $177,000 to $329,000

- Cardiovascular surgeon: $233,500 to $466,000

- Dermatologist: $168,000 to $214,000

- Gastroenterologist: $190,000 to $275,500

- Neurosurgeon: $236,000 to $421,000

- OB-GYN: $175,000 to $245,000

- Oncologist: $172,500 to $292,500

- Ophthalmologist: $170,500 to $247,500

- Orthopedic surgeon: $198,500 to $356,000

- Plastic surgeon: $221,000 to $342,000

- Psychiatrist: $136,000 to $176,000

NURSING

Nurses work all over the country: in small-town hospitals, private clinics, public schools and universities, government public-health agencies, the military, and big-city hospitals. Nurses can work in specialty areas including critical care, the emergency room, maternity, the operating room, pediatrics, and trauma. Others in nursing include nursing educators, nurse epidemiologists, and quality assurance nurses, as well as nursing professionals with Master's degrees (and, typically, higher salaries) such as certified nurse midwives, nurse anesthetists, and nurse practitioners. Some in the field even go on to get their PhD in nursing!

Wherever they are situated, nurses promote the health of their patients. Nurses provide direct patient care in hospitals (which account for two out of three nursing jobs), take care of hospitals' daily regimen of recording patients' vital signs (such as blood pressure), and ensure that medications (including intravenous fluids and other treatments) are administered properly.

Nurses also observe and examine patients, sometimes recommending that a physician investigate a particular problem. And although a large part of a nurse's job is to follow physicians' orders, nurses also have duties separate from those of a doctor.

Unlike doctors, who generally work to cure a specific ailment, nurses concern themselves with a patient's entire well-being. They spend time consulting patients about their diet, hygiene, and the best way to administer patients' medications. Nurses working outside of hospitals don't necessarily deal with the same problems, but they still advise patients, families, and communities on a variety of health-care issues.

Nurses need to be compassionate. They also need to understand complex scientific principles relating to biology and physiology, and work with increasingly complicated medical equipment. And they need to be able to accept responsibility and follow directions precisely.

The outlook for new RNs is exceptionally good; the number of new jobs for registered nurses is expected to increase at a rate far greater than that of most other jobs in coming years. But hospitals, which currently employ the most RNs, won't be where many of the new opportunities develop. Instead, RNs will increasingly find work outside hospitals in home-health and ambulatory care and in nursing homes. Similarly, licensed practical nurses and nurses' aides should also expect to find more opportunities outside of hospitals.

Registered Nurse

RNs assess their patients' conditions, administer medications, interpret and carry out physicians' orders, and make sure their patients are comfortable and being taken care of properly.

Yet registered nurses don't all do the same job; RNs' responsibilities can vary depending on the type and size of the facility at which they work. As one industry insider puts it, "A scrub nurse who works in an operating room might never deal with patients while they're awake. As you can imagine, their job is quite different from the nurse who works in outpatient surgery and on a daily basis is interacting with patients face-to-face to make sure they're recovering and comfortable."

One of the fastest-growing segments of nursing is home-health nursing. Often employed by private agencies or hospitals, home-health nurses visit a patient's home to assess his or her condition and carry out instructions prescribed by the patient's physician.

Nursing homes are also employing registered nurses in increasing numbers, due to a surging elderly population suffering from a disparate range of illnesses associated with ageing. In nursing homes, registered nurses generally carry out supervisory tasks, administrative duties, assess medical conditions, and develop treatment plans to make sure basic health needs are being met.

Other employers of registered nurses include clinics, surgical centers, emergency rooms, health maintenance organizations (HMOs); government and private agencies where nurses instruct people on health education, nutrition, child care, and disease prevention; and schools and companies that require on-site nurses to care for students or employees.

Fifty years ago, virtually all registered nurses working in hospitals were graduates of hospital nursing programs. Such "diploma schools" generally required 3 years of study. Then, in 1952, when the Korean War precipitated a need for more nurses, associate degree programs were introduced. Such programs, primarily administered by community and technical colleges, require 2 years of study outside of the hospital setting. In 1965, however, the American Association of Nurses called for all nurses to get 4-year degrees from universities.

All three routes to becoming a registered nurse have survived. Today, however, hospital programs are greatly on the wane. Currently, about two-thirds of all RNs come from associate programs and the other third from 4-year degree programs.

Once school's finished, you'll have to meet your state board of nursing's requirements and pass the NCLEX-RN exam.

Salary range: $34,000 to $70,000

Nurse Practitioner

NPs work in a wide range of settings, from large hospitals to small clinics to individual practices, administering pediatric care, generally to poorer patients. NPs perform many tasks previously handled only by doctors, such as diagnosing patients. In most states, NPs also have prescription-writing privileges. Nurses must complete a 2-year graduate program to become an NP.

Salary range: $55,000 to $100,000

Licensed Practical Nurse

Licensed practical nurses (LPNs) (also known as licensed vocational nurses) who work in hospitals carry out basic bedside care such as taking temperatures, preparing and giving injections, and collecting blood and fluid samples. LPNs who work in clinics or doctors' offices may also have to complete basic administrative tasks, such as making appointments and keeping records.

LPNs work under the direct supervision of physicians or registered nurses and generally make many fewer decisions than RNs. However, they generally have more responsibilities than nurses' aides and in most states are allowed to administer prescription medications.

To become a licensed practical nurse, you'll need to complete a state-approved practical nursing program. Such programs are generally offered at community and technical colleges and last 1 to 2 years. Then you'll need to pass a state-administered licensing examination. Again, each state has its own rules and regulations.

Salary range: $23,000 to $44,000

OTHER HEALTH-CARE JOBS

Acupuncturist

Acupuncturists work to trigger the body's own natural tendencies toward self-healing by the stimulation of specific points on the patient's body. These points lie on distinct channels or interconnected pathways referred to as meridians. According to the theory behind acupuncture, pain or illness results when the normal flow of energy in the body is disrupted. By stimulating meridians via specific points on the skin, acupuncture eliminates disruption and restores balance. (Modern medicine's best explanation for how acupuncture works is that it stimulates the nervous system, releasing chemicals in the muscles, spinal cord, and brain. These chemicals, which include endorphins, help the body to influence its internal system for regulating pain.)

The range of conditions acupuncture treats runs the gamut from anxiety to sports injury. In conjunction with these traditional treatments, various herbal remedies and dietary adjustments or modifications in lifestyle, such as exercise may be advised.

Acupuncture academic programs vary in length and focus, but most take 3 or 4 years of study and clinical experience. States each maintain their own individual licensing standards.

Salary range: $55,000 to $150,000

Audiologist

Audiologists measure hearing levels in people of all ages. Over half of them work in hospitals, physicians' offices, and schools; others work in hearing aid stores, or conduct scientific research with state and local governments. Finally, a small percentage work in private practice, providing services in their own offices or working under contract for schools and other facilities. An audiology career typically requires a Master's degree, and in 2007 a new standard will require a Ph.D. to practice. Communication skills are an important component of the good audiologist's skill set, since an important part of the job is to communicate diagnostic results and proposed treatments to patients and other health care professionals.

Salary range: $45,000 to $55,000

Clinical Researcher

Researchers work in myriad settings—including hospitals and research organizations—some of them nonprofits. They may work on anything from developing and doing clinical testing on new drugs to developing or conducting tests such as pap smears, HIV screens, and cholesterol tests. Clinical research associate (CRA) positions are one of many typically open to graduates with science backgrounds, including nursing or medicine. Researchers have varying educational backgrounds. Most of them have advanced degrees—from Master's to doctoral levels.

Salary range: $48,000 to $80,000

Dental Assistant

Dental assistants support dentists and dental hygienists as they treat patients. They also perform a range of office-related functions, as well as preparing molds for impressions, processing X-rays, applying topical anesthetics to gums, maintaining dental records, and filling other standard office support functions. Training to become a dental assistant generally takes about a year. Some dental assistants go on to become dental hygienists.

Salary range: $8.45 to $19.41 per hour

Dental Hygienist

Dental hygienists remove soft and hard deposits from teeth, offer additional preventive dental-care services, and educate people in oral hygiene practices. Hygienists examine patients' teeth and gums, recording the presence of diseases or abnormalities. They also do things like take and develop dental X-rays and apply cavity-preventive agents such as fluorides and pit and fissure sealants. In some states, hygienists administer anesthetics; place and carve filling materials, temporary fillings, and periodontal dressings; remove sutures; and smooth and polish metal restorations. Although hygienists are not qualified to diagnose diseases, they can prepare clinical and laboratory tests for the dentist to interpret. Hygienists occasionally work beside dentists during treatment procedures. Hygienists may work in more than one dental office.

Salary range: $17.34 to $25.59 per hour

Dietician

Dieticians (or nutritionists) prepare meal plans and consultations in hospital settings, nursing care facilities, physicians' offices, or home-care settings. Dietitians manage food service systems for institutions such as hospitals and schools, promote sound eating habits through education, and conduct research.

Salary range: $40,800 to $60,000

Home Health Aide

Nursing aides in home care assist patients at their homes instead of inside health facilities. Working under the direction of a nurse or social worker, they administer medications and various related services. They read patients' vital signs, and help them with basic mobility as they go about their daily functions while recuperating from illnesses. Often home aides provide assistance with elderly or injured people requiring more extensive assistance their friends or family can give them. They generally work under the supervision of a doctor, nurse, or other care manager.

The home care aide career is known for its low wages, heavy physical as well as emotional demands, and lack of opportunities for advancement without substantial training. The flexibility to work part-time makes this position appealing for those with other responsibilities, such as families. Training required: a high school diploma, plus a credential, depending on the state.

Salary range: $5.90 to $10.67 per hour

Informatics Specialist

Health-care informatics is one of the fastest-evolving subfields uniting the disciplines of health care, computer science, and information technology (IT) in order to manage and communicate health-care data and knowledge. These days, just about every health-care process that can is becoming automated. For example, patient records (including such enormous items as X-rays) are now digitized, meaning they can be made available almost instantly to others around the globe. In essence, informatics specialists design and manage health-care systems.

Salary range: $35,000 to more than $100,000

Medical Assistant

Medical assistants are typically the first staff to meet patients when they enter a medical office or clinic. Major responsibilities of medical assistants include taking basic readings such as temperature and blood pressure, recording patient medical histories, providing medication, and conferring with the attending physician. They also perform basic administrative functions such as billing, record-keeping, and patient scheduling. This job is one of the fastest-growing in health care

Salary range: $21,620 to $24,460

Medical Records and Health Information Technicians

One of the few health-care occupations with little or no contact with patients, records professionals use computers and specialized software packages to code diseases and transcribe patient records. These professionals generally have associates degrees (AA) and have completed coursework in medical terminology, statistics, and sometimes computer sciences. Information technicians are sometimes required to pass a written exam administered by the American Health Information Management Association (AHIMA). Medical records and health information technicians work in hospital settings, as well as in physicians' offices, nursing care facilities, outpatient care centers, and home health-care services. Medical records and health information technicians organize and evaluate patients' medical records for completeness and accuracy.

Salary range: $21,000 to $26,000

Occupational Therapist

Occupational therapists provide vocational, educational, rehabilitation, physical, emotional, and related services aimed at helping patients acquire, reacquire, and maintain daily living skills.

Most OTs work inside hospitals. Some 82,000 of these practitioners are employed in the United States. They must complete supervised clinical internships in a variety of health-care settings, and pass a national examination; also, most states regulate occupational therapy practices. OT practitioners' education includes the study of human growth and development, with specific emphasis on the social, emotional, and physiological effects of illness and injury. Examples of the kinds of patient problems the OT might deal with include work-related injuries, like lower back problems or repetitive stress injuries; chronic problems such as multiple sclerosis, birth-based injuries, developmental disabilities, learning difficulties, stroke, heart attack, or arthritis; and mental health or behavioral problems include Alzheimer's, schizophrenia, and post-traumatic stress. Other health issues the OT might encounter include substance abuse, eating disorders, burns, spinal cord injuries, amputations, and broken bones or other injuries from falls, sports injuries, or accidents.

Salary range: $35,130 to $74,390

Optometrists

Optometrists treat patients' eyes and vision. They make diagnoses and prescribe treatments, including prescription drugs. In addition, they can also perform some preoperative and post-operative care to cataract patients, as well as on those who have had eye surgery (such as laser vision correction). As necessary, they can refer patients to ophthalmologists (eye specialists with MDs) and other specialists with advanced medical training. In order to become licensed, optometrists must earn a doctor of optometry (OD), requiring 4 years of study, and pass a state board exam.

Salary range: $62,030 to $115,550

Pharmacist

In addition to filling prescriptions and dispensing medications, pharmacists also offer dietary-related advise, monitor health progress of patients on medications, offer stress management and asthma consultations, and prepare intravenous and infusion therapies for home use. A number of drug stores have kicked off new initiatives enabling pharmacists to speak with patients more effectively about how to manage chronic diseases or more complex drug programs.

Increasingly, pharmacists are pursuing less traditional pharmacy work. Some are involved in research for pharmaceutical manufacturers, developing new drugs and therapies and testing their effects on people. Others work in marketing or sales, consulting to clients on a drug's intended use, effectiveness, and possible side effects. Some pharmacists also work for health insurance companies, developing pharmacy benefit packages and carrying out cost-benefit analyses on certain drugs. Others are employed by the government, as well as by pharmaceutical associations. Some pharmacists with more advanced credentials are employed full-time or part-time as college faculty, teaching classes and performing research in a wide range of areas.

In addition, pharmacists can be found in research labs working for governments and associations, where they evaluate drug patterns and outcomes for HMOs and hospitals in order to conduct cost-benefit analyses.

The new Medicare-based drug benefit will likely further increase the already high demand for pharmacists, who are scarce in many parts of the United States.

Salary range: $77,050 to $78,270

Physical Therapist

Physical therapists (PTs) work to improve function and mobility and to relieve pain in patients suffering from disease or injury. PTs often prescribe exercise regimens, or may use other techniques such as electrical stimulation or massage. PTs assess the patients' ability to recuperate, and based on that analysis, tailor rehabilitation plans and work with them until they recover, so they can be re-introduced to their occupational roles as well as other activities such as sports.

Salary range: $57,200 to $62,480

Physician Assistant

Physician assistants (PAs) offer health-care services under the supervision of physicians. Depending on state regulations, they may examine patients, order tests and x-rays, make diagnoses, treat injuries, and prescribe medications. PAs provide even more extensive services than many nurse practitioners. They take down progress notes, instruct and counsel patients, and carry out prescribed courses of therapy. They may be charged with managerial responsibilities as well—such as ordering medical and laboratory supplies and equipment, and supervising technicians and medical assistants.

PAs are becoming increasingly common as the de facto principal care providers in rural and inner city clinics, where a physician may be available for only 1 or 2 days each week. All states require that new PAs have completed an accredited, formal education program. In 2002, there were about 133 accredited or provisionally rated courses of study for physician assistants. Most applicants to PA programs hold either Bachelor's or Master's degrees. PAs pursue additional education in a specialty such as surgery, neonatology, or emergency medicine.

Salary range: $64,670 to $77,280

Technologist/Technician

Technologists require background in the life sciences, while technician positions require only an AA degree. Technicians work in numerous specialties, such as cardiology. They spend most of their time focusing on highly specialized tasks (as is the case with emergency medical technicians, for example) or lab work (such as is the case—see below—of radiology). In addition to training, certification may be required, more so in some specialties than for others. Some technicians learn some of their skills on the job. Some even become technologists with years of on-the-job experience and little or no additional schooling. Technician positions typically require a high school degree, as well as a 1- or 2-year specialty training program, plus some industry-specific certification.

Salary range: $20,000 to $65,000

Following are a couple of technologist/technician specialties.

Radiologic technologists and technicians. Technicians specializing in radiology take X-rays and inject non-radioactive administration of tracers into patients' circulatory systems. More advanced professionals may perform involved procedures such as fluoroscopies, which allow doctors to observe soft tissues in the body. Some focus on specialties such as magnetic resonance imaging (MRI) or computed tomography (CT).

CT technologists perform computer-based scans in order to create images revealing cross-sections of patients. MRIs are created by the application of powerful magnets and radio waves, instead of radiation, in order to create images. Traditionally, they have worked in medical and diagnostic labs, but these days, a greater increase is expected in working with doctors and in ambulatory care and educational services based outside of hospitals. Associated technologic specialties include cardiovascular, diagnostic medical sonographic-based, and nuclear medicine technologists.

Approximately 50 percent of these positions are based in hospitals. Most of the rest are employed in physicians' offices, diagnostic and medical labs, and outpatient care centers.

Salary range: $36,490 to $42,470

Cardiovascular technologist. Technologists specializing in cardiology work with doctors and researchers in diagnosing, treating, and studying diseases and problems related to the heart and associated blood vessels. They work with physicians to perform cardiac catheterization procedures entailing the insertion of a tiny tube (catheter) through the blood vessel from a point in the patient's leg into the heart itself. This procedure can help in diagnosing a host of problems. A related part of the procedure involves balloon angioplasty, commonly used to treat blood vessel or heart valve-based blockages without requiring surgery. These technologists collaborate with cardiologists on these procedures and other non-invasive tests, such as those employing ultrasound.

Salary range: $20,920 to $46,570

Real People Profiles

PHYSICAL THERAPIST

Years in business: 26

Age: 44

Education: BSPT

Size of Organization: 3

Salary: $85,000–100,000

Certification: BSPT; NY State doesn't require continuing education. It varies state to state. NY is in "middle range of states in this regard," but is moving toward requiring certification, he feels.

What do you do?

Since I run my own business, I do a little of everything. That means about 80 percent therapy, 20 percent administrative—even taking out the garbage. We have a total of only three physical therapists, and all of us handle the administrative and clinical work ourselves. We have no aides or trainers on staff.

I generally see anywhere from four to ten patients per day.

My brush with fame: I once treated former President Franklin Roosevelt's son, a local resident, when he and his wife had a buggy accident.

What do you like most about your job?

I like shifting gears throughout the day to encompass a really broad range of types of cases into my practice.

Every patient has the potential to make huge strides (no matter how severe the injury, etc.) It continually excites me when I succeed where other PTs may have failed. It's a really moving experience for me to see people dealing with pain everyday recover and take some control over their situations in life.

Another thing I like about my job: In the past, I've traveled on the circuit with the IMSA racecar driving team.

What do you dislike about it?

Dealing with insurance companies can be a pain. They can't seem to understand how to treat top-notch practitioners as partners, not as adversaries; there is no clear delineation in how they handle reimbursements. Health care has changed tremendously in the United States since I entered the profession way back in 1978.

Another challenge I experience is that the flow of patients can be hard to predict, and there are no-shows and unexpected drop-ins.

What do you view as the biggest misconception about your job?

I feel often people view us as being perhaps less skilled than we really are. PTs need to know how to actually diagnose patients before proper treatment can begin. Their skill in this process simply can't be underestimated. Not enough people seem to really understand how much we need to know to do our jobs effectively.

How can someone get a job like yours?

Internships are a common part of many training programs. Often they will lead to a job offer. Interns sometimes get to rotate through various therapy areas—including, for example, spinal, amputee, and sport medicine.

What kind of person truly excels at this job?

He or she is a good troubleshooter and is good at picking out dysfunctional motions in patients. Patience is very important. The best PTs are able to motivate people of widely varying personalities.

DENTAL ASSISTANT

Years in the profession: 15
Age: 40
Education: AA
Salary: $35,000–40,000
Certification: CDA, RDA, CPR, Radiographic License.
Number of employees: 4

What do you do as a Dental Assistant?

I prepare for and see patients before the dentist arrives. My roles include sterilization, working with x-rays, maintenance of instruments and supplies, front desk administration including reception relief, handling insurance matters, dealing with appointments, and some computer work.

How did you get your job?

I found it reading the newspaper. Internships are another good way to go.

What are your career aspirations?

For me, this is it. I've been here 15 years. I'm pretty set here. Some dental assistants decide to become hygienists, but that occupation requires that them to undergo an additional course of study.

What kind of person does really well at your job?

You have to be a people person and have good communications skills, as well as hands-on skills.

What do you like most about your job?

I enjoy working with the patients, and the sometimes-challenging task of calming those who are fearful. I also enjoy my relationships with other members of the dental team.

What do you like least or dislike?

Some of the patients are uncooperative. And then there's the not-so-clean side of the work: for example, such as suctioning off saliva and blood; you have to be really aware of what you are doing, but we do use protective gloves and masks. Some patients don't pay their bills, but I have little direct involvement in dealing with that issue.

What is the biggest misconception about the job of dental assistant?

I think lots of people think our work is just aspirating saliva, but it involves much more than that. You're communicating with patients. Also, you need to be ready in the rare event of a medial emergency. I have taken CPR training to become better prepared.

CARDIAC LAB MANAGER

Years in the profession: 27
Age: 60
Education: BSN
Salary: "six figures"
Certifications: CCRN in critical care, ASLS (advanced course in life-saving)
Number of employees: 5,200

Briefly, what do you do in your work?

I support physicians in their roles as primary researchers in stem cell studies, gene therapy research, etc. I am now in management, so I am no longer at the bedside. I'm responsible for a $10 million budget.

How did you get your job?

I started as a registered nurse in critical care in Missouri, where I was responsible for meeting the regulatory requirements specific to that environment—about sterility, for example. Over the yeas, I moved into coronary care, and from there into the cardiac catheter lab. In the process, I developed and refined my leadership skills.

How do most folks get this kind of job?

For young people aspiring to my position today, I'd say getting an MBA is the way to go. Work on developing your leadership skills. Continue taking courses.

What are your career aspirations?

Well, I will be retiring in a year and a half. Right now I'm excited to be overseeing the construction of four brand new labs in the main hospital. I am responsible for selecting all the equipment; negotiating with contractors; project managers, etc.; and working through the bidding process.

What kind of person does particularly well at your job?

You have to be flexible, ready to take on situations that are constantly changing. Being fast on your feet and being able to make decisions with a cool head are absolutely essential.

What do you like most about your job?

I especially enjoy interacting with patients. Also, it's stimulating working with my colleagues; they are very intense and knowledgeable—extremely clinically adept at what they do.

What, if anything, do you like least or dislike?

The only thing I can think of has to do with the older facility we occupy here at the main building on campus. It lacks some bed capacity.

What is the biggest misconception, in your estimation, about the job of lab manager?

When new managers coming in, they have the perception that the job will be a 9–5, Monday through Friday, job. In fact, it's a lot more intense. I am on call 24 hours a day, 7 days a week: it's a 24x7 situation.

Please describe a typical day.

I start at 7:30 to 8:00 a.m., go to the charge nurse in the cath lab (catheter lab), review outstanding issues or problems of the day, count the available beds in house for the day, and accordingly cancel some outpatients to fit our capacity.

I have administrative meetings throughout the day. They have to do with everything from conscious sedation (once a month) and supply chain (once a week) to divisional nursing issues (once a week) and the ongoing construction initiative on our four new labs (started a couple of years ago). Others revolve around interventional issues (some 50 percent of my time) to the logistics in planning our move to the new facilities. From 5:00–6:00 I return calls and e-mails.

I also evaluate staff members and the $10 million budget for the next fiscal year. Other issues I deal with include resolving patient complaints and touching base with patients and families. I play a liaison role with families.

I usually leave by around 6:00 to 6:30 p.m.

OPTOMETRIST

Age: 36

Education: OD

Salary: $70,000–90,000

Certification: Continuing education is required, entailing 50 credit hours every 2 years by CA state law.

Number of employees: 124

What do you do?

I examine patients' vision. In seeing patients—both new patients and follow-up cases—I also work on minor eye emergencies; for example, a contact might be stuck in an eye, or a person may have red eye or a mild corneal abrasion from a trauma. I make referrals to ophthalmologists on a case-by-case basis.

I also handle administrative responsibilities such as account billing; each OD handles his or her own. I take money to the bank daily. The retail side (optical, lenses, and frames) of our chain is separate from what I do.

What do you like about your job?

It's very personable here, and I especially like working directly with people and feel confidant in what I do; I credit my training in Philadelphia. I like problem-solving and diagnosing symptoms.

What do you dislike about it?

I don't like my long commute into the city from the suburbs. And sometimes patients are very unappreciative. Since it's a small chain, occasionally folks treat us like we're a McDonald's. But I offer the same exact level of care as you'll find in a private practice, which is where I got my experience before coming to work here.

What do you view as the biggest misconception about your job?

I think people feel that the Lasik eye surgery boom will hurt our business, but in fact it could be actually enhancing it. Our company may very well get involved in co-management with Lasik operations someday, and that association would bring us lots of new business. Also, some people don't know that ODs are equipped and trained to treat minor eye problems.

How can someone get a job like yours?

My girlfriend (now wife) found the job listing on the Internet while we were still in Philadelphia. You won't find ads for optometrists that much in newspapers, though. Typically, universities make professional placements.

What are your career aspirations?

That's changed a lot since my wife and I had our first baby. I think that a lot hinges on what would be best for me as a father and husband. I'm uncertain about pursuing management roles—mostly because of concerns about the stress that might result.

What kind of person does really well at this job?

I would say someone with very good communication skills and who really understands the physics behind optics and optical corrections. Someone who can interpret the patients' needs, has good business sense, and is interested in ocular health issues—as well as the medical aspects of treating these kinds of problems.

X-RAY TECHNOLOGIST

Years in business: 12 years
Age: 40
Education: AA degree
Salary: $30–40 per hour
Number of employees: 15
Certification: ARRT for national. CRT for CA

What do you do as an MRI Technician?

I take X-rays, position patients in the MRI machine, program the scans, and monitor the scans for motion and quality. I also talk to the requesting doctor about the scan to be performed.

It took me 2 and a half years to complete the course of study in X-ray technology. An X-ray license is required to perform MRIs in most states.

What are your career aspirations?

I would like to start my own business.

What kind of person does particularly well at your job?

The right person for this job is someone who cares about people. I have worked with people who just look at this job for a paycheck and treat people like dirt. The main thing about this job is you have to be caring; people coming to you for an X-ray or MRI are in pain. I'm not saying that you have to be an entertainer, but you have to be sensitive as to their particular situation.

What do you like most about your job?

The idea that I can make a difference in somebody's life by the quality of care I give and the extra mile I go in the scans I do. One thing I like about the X-ray field is that there are so many other avenues that are open to you with an X-ray license.

The main think I have learned working in this clinic and a couple of hospitals and trauma center is that I'm very fortunate. When you see shooting victims, car accident victims, suicide attempt victims, cancer patients, mental patients, you realize this is real, not a TV show you can turn off if you don't like what you see. I wouldn't discourage anybody about this job, because it's been great, but sometimes you have to have a real strong stomach to deal with what comes in the door

What is the biggest misconception about the job of MRI Technician?

The patients expect you to read the MRIs. Since I'm not a radiologist, I cannot read the MRIs.

Describe a typical day.

The day starts at 8:00 and I do a test scan in about 5 minutes. I then check the patient list for MRI reports from the previous day. All MRIs should have been read the day before. My patients are scheduled every hour on the hour. I have them fill out a pre-screening form for any metal in their body, ask them some basic questions, and put them in the MRI scanner. When the scan is finished, I pull them out and send the scan by e-mail to the radiologist to read. Then I go to the next patient.

On a typical patient day, I see 10–25 patients and work 8 hours. On non-patient days, I work 8 hours or more.

NURSE PRACTITIONER

Age: 31

Education: BSN (Bachelor of Science in Nursing); MSN (Master of Science in Nursing)

Salary: $60,000–83,000

Certification: Glide requires national nursing certification entitled ANCC (American Nurses Credentialing Center), or AANP (American Academy of Nurse Practitioners). The initial certification requires an examination. To keep up with the latest treatment guidelines and advances we do some home study, attend seminars, etc.

What do you do?

I was originally trained as a registered nurse, and I did that for about 7 years. Presently, I work as a nurse practitioner in community clinic settings. I now work at both Glide Health Clinic and Tenderloin AIDS Resource Center. I prefer my present work to my prior job as clinical RN. Lots of doctors are still not aware of what nurse practitioners can do. With my background, I am prepared to work in primary care as well as perform some mental-health functions.

I feel the role of nurse practitioner is evolving, and expect it to grow even more in demand within next the 20–30 years. The trend is upward due to a projected shortage of doctors to care for the growing elder population, and the aging of doctors, as well.

What do you like about your job?

What I like the most about my job is having the opportunity to work with people to try to prevent them from becoming sick and being hospitalized. More specifically, I enjoy educating people about their chronic illnesses so they can be equipped to have better control over their lives.

What do you dislike about it?

The challenge I experience is that the flow is hard to predict, and there are no-shows and unexpected drop-ins. I generally see anywhere from four to ten patients per day.

What do you view as the biggest misconception about your job?

That I can't perform many of the functions that a physician does. There are limitations to what I can do in certain settings, but in the clinics that I work in I am pretty much able to do everything that a physician does. This issue usually comes up when I don't give clients what they want. They get upset and say, I want to see a doctor.

How can someone get a job like yours?

In order to get a job as a nurse practitioner, you have to first be a licensed registered nurse. The next step is to complete an MSN program, and apply for state licensure.

What are your career aspirations?

I have an interest in doing many things as a nurse practitioner. I enjoy working with persons who have mental health and substance abuse issues. I am also interested in working with persons who are incarcerated. I enjoy having the opportunity to teach people who are training to become nurses. In the future, I think that I would like to teach at a university and/or open a private practice of some sort.

What kind of person does really well at this job?

Someone who is flexible, has a sense of humor, has the ability to be compassionate but firm, and is good at thinking quick on their feet.

Please describe a typical day.

I arrive to the clinic between 8:30 and 9:00 am. I work in the walk-in-center doing health screenings, health consultations, giving immunizations, refilling medications, and referring clients to health services if necessary. While in the walk-in-center, I also provide treatment for minor injuries (e.g., cuts or abrasions) and provide treatment for lice and scabies.

I take a lunch break in the afternoon. After lunch, I work in the clinic doing primary care. I usually see four patients, but if there are drop-in appointments, I may have to see five patients per day. People come in for a variety of reasons: routine care of their chronic conditions (diabetes, hypertension, etc.), urgent care for pain caused from injuries . . . some people come in with urgent mental health issues, and others come in to have physical exams as a requirement for employment or school.

Depending on the types of patients coming in, my level of stress fluctuates. But overall, I always feel a sense of accomplishment at the end of the day.

STAFF PHARMACIST

Years in the profession: 20
Age: 45
Education: PharmD
Salary: $38,310 (half-time)
Certification: State Board Pharmacy classes, but no tests administered.
Number of employees: 40,000

What do you do as a staff pharmacist?

I screen patients for any specific health issues or problems before preparing the prescription. It involves a lot of insurance-related issues.

How did you get your job?

I sent my resume to the hospital after seeing an ad in the newspaper. I live in a city and like working in a central location.

What are your career aspirations?

I am happy to continue working part-time. I like the flexibility.

What kind of person does really well at your job?

A people-oriented, patient, efficient person with strong time-management skills.

What do you like most about your job?

I enjoy working with the patients and my fellow staff; we get along very well.

What do you like least or dislike?

There are lots of legal issues to deal with, and laws are constantly changing. I feel stuck in the middle.

What is the biggest misconception about the job of staff pharmacist?

What I actually do is much more involved than what the average person might think. A large part of our work involves screening. We are continually studying to keep up on the latest pharmaceuticals, as well as continuing education to maintain our licensures. The stress level is pretty constant. There's a heavy workload, and lives are at stake if we do something even slightly off.

Describe a typical day.

I work some days in the outpatient pharmacy and other days in the inpatient hospital pharmacy across the street, in which I work more closely to where the patients are being treated. Although the protocols are very different, neither job is really any more difficult than the other.

PEDIATRICIAN

Years in the profession: 16
Age: 44
Education: BA., M.D.
Salary Range: $150,000–180,000
Company size: 150,000

What do you do as Pediatrician?

Currently, I treat mainly adolescents. That's the age group of greatest personal interest to me. A few years ago I started a teen clinic at another hospital. In my work, I enjoy a fair amount of variety. My specialty working with adolescents gives me an interesting perspective on children's rights as patients. For example, certain parts of their records—such as that having to do with sexually transmitted diseases—even their parents can't access.

I give high school students check-ups, work with medical students from osteopathic schools and nurse practitioner (NP) students doing rotations in my area, and attend continuing education meetings once a week. We rotate topics of discussion around such topics as medicine for pediatrics, elder care, obesity, and pain management—which is one of the bigger issues we address.

I am a consultant on a project revolving around computerization of patient records for my hospital. Since I work 4 days a week, I actually have a good deal of flexibility in my schedule throughout the month.

How did you get your job?

After getting my MD in NY, I did a residency at my present employer, the same company that owns the hospital where I was born.

What are your career aspirations?

I was honored to join the HMO's subcommittee (pediatrics) on e-medicine to plan for the future. We are developing new templates for care in our region—and in so doing, charting the frontiers of electronic medicine of the future.

It's exciting to play a key role in the digitization of patient records because I have seen first-hand how it is improving the effectiveness of our services over the years.

What kind of person does particularly well at your job?

You have to love children and have great patience with them, as well as with new parents.

What do you like most about your job?

I like working with kids and getting to know families as they grow up together. That's important.

What, if anything, do you like least or dislike?

Every now and then it becomes so incredibly busy. But that's not very often. Back in the mid-90's our hospital was experiencing lots of problems, and for a while we had to work half a day each week without pay. But where I work, physicians are salaried, so we get the same pay regardless of how many patients we see.

What is the biggest misconception, in your estimation, about the job of pediatrician?

Some think that when a doctor like myself takes care of kids, you're not communicating with them but with their parents. In fact, kids are great communicators! Also, people sometimes think you don't have a life, another untrue notion.

ASSISTANT PROFESSOR OF MEDICINE

Years in the profession: 7
Age: 36
Education: BA., M.D.
Salary: $90,000–160,000
Certifications: USMLE (Medical Licensing), Board Certification of Internal Medicine & Cardiology
Number of employees: 5,200

What do you do?

My contract says that I am to do research 80 percent of the time and patient care 20 percent. In reality, it is more like 20 percent patients, 65 percent research, and 15 percent teaching and administration. I teach at all levels—from 1st-year to 4th-year medical students, interns and residents, as well as cardiology fellows. My administrative duties involve mainly advising and interviewing. This is what I do for the residency and fellowship programs.

How did you get your job?

Of course, I started by going through medical school. In my case, I was first drawn toward psychiatry, but I was frustrated by the lack of treatment options and gravitated toward areas of medicine where one could have a more immediate impact such as cardiology. My father was an academic cardiologist, and eventually that was the path I chose to pursue, as well. As an undergrad, I majored in psychology and music, and I took very few really tough science courses in college.

In my first year at medical school, I was completely overwhelmed. So I worked in a lab after my first year, and was immediately attracted to the sense of creativity I found there. Also, between my third and fourth years, I took a year and half to do lab work again; for some of that time I got credits for toward my medical school program.

It was there in the lab that I found my mentor. I had the rare experience of finding my sub-specialty of cardiology before formally choosing a specialty (internal medicine).

Most medical students decide which specialties they pursue based on preconceived ideas or on what environments they have been most comfortable in as they progress through medical school. In reality, most students are exposed to a small slice of medical life, mainly via their residencies. Lots of doctors change specialties and jobs at some point in their careers.

What are your career aspirations?

I have several interests, so it is hard offer a simple answer. But most importantly, I like to continue asking and answering interesting questions in everything I do. I am open to the possibility of playing more administrative kinds of roles in the future.

What kind of person does particularly well at your job?

I think my natural child-like sense of curiosity helps—in fact, it is practically essential. The most important thing to acknowledge though, is the tremendous amount of patience involved. Scientific investigation is an inherently slow-moving process.

What do you like most about your job?

I just keep asking myself rhetorically, Am I happier now than I have been earlier? I have been fortunate to have had a lot of opportunities to compare my visceral experiences in a lot of areas, and I keep coming back for more.

What, if anything, do you like least or dislike?

The downside is limitless. There's absolutely no job security. The issue of funding is the perhaps the most difficult challenge of my job. At first, a little cushion or leash is given, but then we need to write grants. But, I know it could end at any moment.

Lots of luck and capriciousness is involved. I'm concerned about the trend toward less funding (from the NIH, for example) for research over the past 10–15 years. In the old days, academic divisions gave support. These days it's a different story. Someone else (anywhere in the country) could have discovered what I just did—literally moments before my work. But that's what makes it so challenging. Mostly, I'm intensely curious about how things work.

I'm noticing that more folks are being drawn toward areas requiring less personal sacrifice in term of years of preparation, etc. It took me 12 years after obtaining my BA degree. That concerns me, too, because fewer folks are getting into research than was the case 20–30 years ago.

Also, I'm concerned about health insurance-related issues and about the crisis of reimbursements. We are witnessing a trend toward doctors exclusively accepting cash instead of insurance to avoid having to deal with this painful issue.

What is the biggest misconception, in your estimation, about the role of medical school professor?

That's difficult to answer. I don't think anyone (except my wife) totally understands what I do. When I tell someone I'm a professor or medicine, most don't have any idea what I do. Partly, that's because I wear lots of hats.

The Workplace

Lifestyle

Culture

Workplace Diversity

Compensation, Benefits, and Vacation

Training

Career Path

Insider Scoop

Lifestyle

The lifestyle of health-care professionals can vary greatly, depending on a variety of factors—everything from job title, practice specialty, and career stage to geographic location, type of facility, and organization type.

Early in their careers, doctors are notorious for working the kinds of hours that would, well, put other people in the hospital. We've all heard the stories of residents who have had to spend 72 straight hours in the hospital—the tales of young, on-call doctors who sneak catnaps in the janitor's closet, and the likes. Later in their careers, different doctors can have vastly different lifestyles, with some working 40 hours a week, and others twice or three times that.

Nurses and most other health-care practitioners are much more likely to work more normal-sounding hours. And because of high demand for their services, many nurses, home health aides, and other health-care practitioners usually have the opportunity to create part-time careers.

The lifestyle can vary by what part of the country you're in, too. Working in an emergency room in an inner-city neighborhood, for instance, can involve quite a lot more action, stress, and potential for long hours than does the typical ER shift in a quiet, well-to-do hospital—as can working in an understaffed hospital in a poor rural area.

There is no "typical" lifestyle in health care. If you're an introvert, you might prefer working in research. If you want to work with people, you might want to be a nurse, or a physical therapist, or . . . you get the idea.

But while health-care industry lifestyles can differ enormously, in general, health-care work involves dealing with a fast pace of new demands on your attention and a sense of urgency to get things done—and get them done right.

In general, most health-care jobs don't demand much in the way of travel, other than your commute to work. But those who enter the business or entrepreneurial side of health care may find themselves on the road a good deal in order to attend association meetings and establish and nurture relationships with client organizations.

Culture

There are as many different types of workplace cultures in health care as there are patients. After all, this industry comprises everything from sports medicine clinics (which tend to treat younger, more active patients) and pediatrician's offices (which treat children) to long-term Alzheimer's-care facilities (which treat the elderly more often than not). You might work alone (e.g. the solo-practitioner psychotherapist); you might work in a small office (e.g. an internal-medicine clinic); or you might work in a giant institution (e.g. an HMO or large hospital network). You might work in a hospital with a Catholic affiliation; you might work in a hospital with a Jewish affiliation. And so on. Accordingly, you're going to find a wide range of cultures in this industry.

However, there are some things that are fairly common to most health-care workplace cultures. For one, most health-care organizations function as pretty rigid hierarchies, in terms of responsibilities and reporting structure. When you're a nurse, for instance, you know that you can't prescribe treatments; only a doctor or maybe a nurse practitioner can do that.

In addition, there's the bureaucracy. The stereotypical health-care organization is big and slow-moving. The stereotype exists because there's a lot of truth to it. Even at many smaller health-care organizations, which don't suffer from the type of bureaucracy that comes with size, there always seems to be more and more insurance-related paperwork to take care of. That's not to say there aren't small, nimble health-care organizations out there, for those of you with a more entrepreneurial bent (or a need for a flatter org chart), only that filling out paperwork and following procedure is a big part of life at most health facilities.

And then there's the stress level. While there are exceptions, at most types of health-care facilities, the relentless demand for greater and greater efficiency has created a high-stress culture. Health-care professionals at all levels are being asked to handle more responsibility, complete more tasks, and, often, work longer hours than was the case a generation ago.

The culture at many health-care organizations can also come with a healthy dollop of fear. Due to the explosion in malpractice insurance litigation over the past generation, many doctors, for instance, work in constant fear that they'll be sued and lose all the wealth they've worked to attain. And as the industry consolidates, at many institutions (especially those that are attractive takeover targets) folks at all levels run scared of being laid off.

All that said, there are still many, many places in this industry with excellent workplace cultures. At the best health-care employers, people have a sense that they're doing valuable work for their community, and take pride in that fact. Many health-care employers have excellent benefits packages, to boot. Both those things are under fire in the industry due to the growing focus on the bottom line—and to the resulting demand for lower costs and higher profits. You may find a less cost-cutting-focused culture in private employers, though even there the trend is toward cutting costs and doing more with less. Still, there are excellent employers in the industry; for example, the 2006 *Fortune* list of the "100 Best Places to Work" included Griffin Hospital (in Connecticut), Vision Service Plan (California), Baptist Health Care (Florida), Baptist Health South Florida, Northwest Community Healthcare (Illinois), Memorial Health (Georgia), Bronson Healthcare Group (Michigan), Children's Healthcare of Atlanta, Methodist Hospital System (Texas), and the Mayo Clinic (Minnesota).

Workplace Diversity

In general, health care is a very diverse industry, with health-care facilities employing a mix of people similar to that of the community where they're located. That's especially true at large facilities, like hospitals; at smaller facilities, you might find less diversity than you'd expect. And in some careers, you might encounter an under-representation of various groups. For instance, there are about twice as many male doctors as female. (This is changing, however; in 2004, for example, more women applied for medical school than men, for the second straight year.) And in most parts of the country, if you're a man, you won't have much company of your own gender among the nursing staff where you work.

Compensation, Benefits, and Vacation

Compensation, benefits, and vacation policy can vary by job title, organization type, organization size, geographic location, career stage, and the likes. At the lower end of the spectrum, a home-health aide might make less than $10 bucks an hour; at the higher end, a successful surgeon in a major metropolitan area can make more than $1 million per year. In general, for trained professionals, the health-care sector pays fairly well. Following are some sample salary ranges from the Bureau of Labor Statistics.

Typical Salary Ranges in Health Care

Profession	Salary Range
Anesthesiologist	$206,000–295,000
Cardiologist	$177,000–329,000
Cardiovascular surgeon	$233,500–466,000
Cytotechnologist	$50,000–56,000
Dermatologist	$168,000–214,000
Emergency medical technician/paramedic	$21,000–26,000
Family practice MD	$128,000–163,000
Gastroenterologist	$190,000–275,500
Home health aide	$17,000–20,500
Licensed practical nurse	$35,000–40,000
Medical assistant	$25,000–30,000
Medical laboratory technician	$30,000–36,000
Medical technologist	$44,000–50,500
Neurosurgeon	$236,000–421,000
Nurse practitioner	$65,700–76,500
OB-GYN	$175,000–245,000
Occupational therapist	$53,350–61,250
Oncologist	$172,500–292,500
Ophthalmologist	$170,500–247,500
Optician	$34,150–41,000
Optometrist	$85,500–96,000
Orthopedic surgeon	$198,500–356,000
Pharmacist	$86,000–96,500
Physical therapist	$55,000–65,000
Physician assistant	$65,000–75,000
Phlebotomist	$22,500–26,500
Plastic surgeon	$221,000–342,000
Podiatrist	$84,750–158,000
Psychiatrist	$136,000–176,000
Radiologic technologist	$39,500–45,500
Registered nurse	$50,750–60,000

Training

Many health-care professions require specialized education and/or training, and/or licensure from the government. Doctors, for instance, must be licensed by the state in which they practice. Degrees are granted to graduates of accredited medical schools who have passed a licensing exam (the USMLE, United States Medical Licensing Examination) and completed 1 to 7 years of graduate medical school (residency) in an accredited program. Most specialists also become board certified in their specialty in order to gain an edge in a competitive job market, though board certification is not a state requirement.

Accredited medical schools are those that have been approved by the Liaison Committee on Medical Education (LCME). A list of accredited medical programs is available at LCME's website. Accredited residency programs have been approved by the Accreditation Council for Graduate Medical Education (ACGME). A list of accredited residencies is available on the ACGME's site.

Nurses can become qualified through hospital nursing programs, generally requiring 3 years of study, associate degree programs at community or technical colleges, usually completed within 2 years, or 4-year university degree programs. Hospital programs are greatly on the wane. Currently, about two-thirds of all RNs come from associate programs and the other third from 4-year degree programs.

Once school's finished, you'll have to meet your state board of nursing's requirements and pass the NCLEX-RN exam.

There's been some talk about splitting up the field of nursing into "professional nurses," for those who have 4-year degrees, and "technical nurses," for those with associate degrees. North Dakota even went so far as to require a 4-year bachelor's degree, and other states may follow suit. Currently, however, either route can lead you to a job as a staff nurse at a hospital.

Some jobs in nursing—such as a position as a public health nurse—require the 4-year degree. Plus, hospitals are more likely to promote a staff nurse with a college degree to a supervisory (and higher paying) role. And finally, to become an advanced practice nurse—such as a nurse practitioner or certified nurse anesthetist, you have to have a bachelor's degree first.

With a bachelor's degree out of the way, graduate school is open to nurses who want to climb the career ladder and get an advanced-practice degree. Most degrees require an extra 2 to 3 years of postgraduate study. Once that's done, you'll need to pass a national examination to become certified.

To become a licensed practical nurse, you'll need to complete a state-approved practical nursing program. Such programs are generally offered at community and technical colleges and last 1 to 2 years. Then you'll need to pass a state-administered licensing examination. Again, each state has its own rules and regulations.

Teaching hospitals employ many of the MD and nursing trainees. But people in other jobs and/or types of health-care organizations may also face education/training and/or licensure or certification requirements. Medical technicians, for instance—such as MRI technicians—may require specialized training. Even over on the business side of the industry, certain jobs might require IT certification, for instance, or an MBA degree.

Career Path

Many career paths in health care are fairly predictable. You do your job, and continue to do it until you get certified to do a higher-paying version of your job, but with greater responsibility. (Consider: Med students move on to become interns, who move on to become residents, who move on to work in fellowships, in an HMO, PPO, and/ or hospital, and/or in private practice. Similarly, nurse's aides often study to become licensed practical nurses, some of whom study to become registered nurses, some of whom study to become nurse practitioners. . . .)

While some doctors pursue advancement into management positions, most simply continue to practice medicine. As a doctor's career advances, he or she will typically develop a base of regular patients and accept fewer new ones. The heavy workloads and long hours of a doctor's early career will also generally slow down as the doctor approaches retirement.

Similarly, many nurses move into part-time positions once they have the responsibilities of a family; the ever-strengthening demand for nurses means that flexibility will probably continue to be a benefit of nursing careers in coming years.

These days, doctors, nurses, and other health-care professionals enjoy more professional options than ever before. Nurses are often hired into consulting firms, for instance, and many MDs move over to the business side of the industry; some MDs even become entrepreneurs, starting various medicine- and health-related ventures.

Insider Scoop

WHAT'S GREAT

Feels Good to Make Others Feel Good

Even if your medical career has only gone as far as plumping pillows and soothing a fevered brow, you can probably sense why the many dedicated people in this industry continue to selflessly perform often-menial labor for scant compensation and recognition. Recent studies have shown that HMO technicians and doctors rate their job satisfaction significantly lower than that of nurses, aides, and therapists who care for the sick—often with significantly less pecuniary reward.

Need Flexibility?

One former teacher recalls arriving in a small town in Florida with little chance of finding work in the local schools. Finally, in desperation, she took a part-time job at a nursing home and discovered a whole new career. "I really love my work," she says. With 5 years' experience under her belt, she says, "I make my own hours, and I'm earning very good money." Many people who fall into this field stay put because they can better balance the demands of family, school, and other commitments—both with more ease and associated emotional rewards than is the case with most other kinds of part-time work.

Goodbye, Rusty Saw

Advances in medical technology over the last 30 years have been truly phenomenal. The same patients who were once read their last rites are now routinely patched up and returned to healthy, productive lives—often with procedures that can be handled on an outpatient basis. Whether or not you're a researcher at heart, playing an integral role in the ongoing medical revolution can be immensely personally rewarding and intellectually stimulating.

WHAT'S TO HATE

Care for Profit?

Most people pursue a career in care because they want to help people in need. Increasingly, however, the business side of health care has come between patients and providers. "At my hospital, we're supposed to call the patients 'customers'," says one insider. "I keep telling my boss this is not Lord & Taylor!" or "All I can say is it stinks, and corporate America has no business in the system," says another. Lots of strong emotions emerge in this discussion, and these days are certainly not easy or happy ones in this industry. The higher up the ladder you go, the more bruising and harsh the politics and economics tend to become.

The 15-Minute Consultation

With or without the capable assistance of a PA or NP, about 15 minutes is about how much time most physicians are allocated per patient these days. Think about it. If a patient showed up with searing pains in her legs, and two previous doctors apparently were not providing immediate assistance, how would you feel about giving yet another cursory inspection and diagnosis? Everyone's complaints, no matter how seemingly routine, deserve focus and attention. Most health-care professionals feel this even more strongly than their patients do. Physician practice management groups (PPMs) are proliferating and becoming increasingly vocal in their angry opposition to the heavy, restrictive hand of managed care. This is a problem that will likely get worse before it gets better.

Pressures on Nurses

The downside (there's always a downside, isn't there?) of the nursing shortage becomes clear once you accept one of those high-paying jobs. Because of staffing shortages, people in nursing are finding themselves saddled with increasing numbers of patients to care for. In some organizations today, nurses are under significant pressure to work overtime.

Survival of the Fattest

Insiders readily acknowledge the fact that the poor receive a different standard of health care. Some would argue that for the richest nation in the world to be without a federally subsidized health program, particularly for the indigent, is unconscionable. Others insist that a rigorous level of medical excellence can only be maintained as a well-run, competitive business. It's troubling to everyone, though, that those most vulnerable to both chronic and emergency illness are those with fewer and fewer available avenues of recourse to fairly priced quality health care.

Getting Hired

The Recruiting Process

Requirements

Interviewing Tips

Getting Grilled

Grilling Your Interviewer

The Recruiting Process

The recruiting process in health care varies by organization, job function, and career stage. Smaller health care providers—for example, the office of a family practice doctor—don't really do much in terms of recruiting, other than placing help-wanted ads in the window when they need new bodies. Larger organizations are more likely to have more formal recruiting programs and processes.

Take registered nurses. A smaller health-services provider organization will typically hire whatever nurses it needs via classified ads, or perhaps by contracting with a nursing recruiting firm. (Nurses entering the job market are well advised to do some research to learn whether there are any nurse recruiters in their area who can help them find the job they want.) A larger organization might also find nurses via third-party recruiters, but it is also likely to have formal recruiting programs to recruit nurses itself. For instance, it might have a presence at local health services–related job fairs. And/or it might have a relationship with a local nursing school, through which it hires the bulk of its new nurses. (In the case of a university hospital, the nursing school and the hiring institution might be part of the same organization.)

Of course, as in any other field, networking can be the best way to find the job you want in health care.

Requirements

Again, because this is such a huge industry, employing so many different kinds of workers, there's no such thing as typical requirements for health-care job candidates. For example, clinical research positions require more hard-sciences education than do nurse's aides, and nurses often need to be more nurturing than doctors in their dealings with patients. And a marketing or finance position at an HMO might entail an entirely different set of skills, education, and experience.

In many cases—consider MDs and RNs—health-care workers must undergo a very specific course of education. And many health-care workers require specialized training and/or licensure or certification.

Still, there are a number of personal attributes that will probably serve you well if you decide to go into health care:

- A desire to serve others. At its heart, despite the industry's shift in focus during the past generation from health-care quality to financial performance, in most practitioner jobs in the industry, it's all about helping patients. If it was just about the paycheck, health care workers would look for work in industries with greater pay for less time and hassle.

- Some business sense. Still and all, the fact remains that most health-care organizations are more focused on the bottom line these days than ever. If you can show you understand the business reasons for the strategic and tactical decisions your potential employer makes, you'll be more likely to get the job.

- Grace under pressure. A lot of practitioner jobs count an ability to deal with stress, and an ability to make decisions on the fly, among the skills required for the job.

- An ability and desire to work hard.

Interviewing Tips

KNOW YOUR TARGET EMPLOYERS

No matter what kind of job you're looking for in health care, you can only help your chances of landing the job you want by becoming more informed. First, of course, you should know everything you can about any organization you're interviewing with: how it has performed of late, the challenges facing it, its strategy moving forward, and so on. Read about the organization on its website, in its annual report, in the business press. Prospective employers are always impressed when an interviewee exhibits this kind of knowledge; it shows a real interest in the company.

Beyond that, you should also understand what's happening among your prospective employer's competition: What are the big trends in the industry, and so on? How is your prospective employer performing relative to its competition, and why? Of course, if you're interviewing with a prospective employer that's not doing so well versus the competition, you'll want to focus not on how and why the prospective employer is performing poorly vis-à-vis competitors in your interviews, but on potential solutions to challenges it's facing.

Finally, you'll need a thorough understanding of and interest in the type of work you'll be doing, for two reasons:

1) If you aren't interested in the kind of work you'll be doing, chances of you loving your job are much lower.

2) If you can convincingly convey your enthusiasm for an organization and for your place in it, you'll be much more likely to persuade that organization to hire you.

PREPARE, PREPARE, PREPARE

In a first-round interview, you may only have 30 minutes to tell your story. You should have at least one example each of leadership, teamwork, analysis, problem solving, how you have dealt with a difficult coworker or patient, and how you learned from a mistake you made. And, of course, you should be able to talk specifics when it comes to questions gauging your skills in and knowledge of the specific career function you're interviewing for; in other words, if you're interviewing for a pediatric nursing job, you'd better be prepared to show that you know the field inside and out.

LISTEN CAREFULLY

Repeat the question at the beginning of your response to confirm that you heard it correctly. You can't afford to spend 3 minutes telling a story, only to have the interviewer say, "That's interesting, but can you answer my question?"

To help you focus on issues that are important to interviewers, frame your answers according to the following outline:

1) Situation

2) Conflict/challenge

3) Action steps

4) Results

Using this format will also help you remember your stories!

PROMOTE YOURSELF

Interviews are not the place to be humble. It may be awkward for you to tell stories that focus more on "I" than on "we," but it is essential that you articulate your specific role in an activity, event, or decision. If all of your examples describe the good work that "we" did, the recruiter will have no idea what "you" did.

CHOOSE YOUR WEAKNESS CAREFULLY

One of the classic interview questions is, "Describe a weakness." This is not the time to confess that you are disorganized or prone to procrastination. One insider reports that the safest answers to this question are either, "I have a tendency to over-commit," or "I have struggled at times with being a workaholic." In both instances, these observations are followed by some variation on ". . . but I'm making progress in that area."

Interviewers, of course, have heard this before, so you may be prodded to name another weakness. Whatever weakness you choose, just be sure it's not directly related to skills that are needed to be effective in the specific career you're interested in; for example, if you're interviewing for a job as a phlebotomist, don't talk about how the sight of blood sometimes make you faint.

BE ENTHUSIASTIC

Leave your pom-poms at home, but be relentlessly upbeat and positive throughout the course of your interview, even if your interviewer seems tired or disinterested. The stone-faced interviewer may be testing you to see how easily you are discouraged.

INTERVIEW COMPANY INSIDERS

Not surprisingly, insiders tell us that the best sources of information about an organization are people who work for it. If you can find a colleague who interned at an organization or an alum who works there now, an informational interview can be enormously useful.

Getting Grilled

GENERAL INTERVIEW QUESTIONS

Following are questions you should be prepared to answer no matter what career function you're interested in.

- What's your biggest strength? Your biggest weakness?

- What appeals to you most about this position?

- Why are you interested in this organization?

- Are you applying at any other organizations? Which ones? (Be prepared to convince the interviewer that this is your top choice, and if the other organizations are strikingly different, be sure you can draw a convincing connection.)

- Can you tell me about a time when you worked on a team with people whose skill sets were markedly different from your own?

- What personality type would you say you have the least in common with? Can you tell me about a time when you worked with such a person?

- Describe how you have resolved a misunderstanding with a coworker in the past.

- Can you describe an ambitious goal you set for yourself and the steps you took to reach it?

- Give me an example of a time you didn't meet your goal for a project. What went wrong?

- Tell me about a time when you assumed a leadership role on a project.

- Have you ever had to finish a project that someone else started? How did you handle that?

- How do you prefer to receive direction from superiors?

- What skills would you expect to hone in this position?

- Where do you see yourself in 5, 10, or 15 years? How do you plan to get there?

- What would you say are the three trends shaping the health care industry? How should smart health-care organizations respond to these trends?

Grilling Your Interviewer

The question period at the end of the interview can be very important. You can leave a favorable impression by asking tough but thoughtful questions. Failing to ask questions suggests either that you're not seriously interested in the position or that you are not a critical thinker.

You'll need to prepare some questions of your own, but we've drawn up some sample questions. Those in the "Rare" section are meant to be innocuous, whereas the "Well Done" questions will put a fire to your interviewer's feet. Use the "Well Done" questions at your own risk.

RARE

- What health-care providers do you consider the most innovative, and why?

- What kinds of changes have you seen since you've been with the organization?

- What types of community service and philanthropic activities does the organization participate in?

MEDIUM

- How is the culture of your organization different from that of its competitors?

- What training opportunities are available?

- How have you personally made a difference at the organization?

WELL-DONE

- What is the most common reason people give for leaving this job? This organization?

- What does the organization do really well?

- What does the organization need to work on?

- If you could change three things about the organization (or this particular department within the organization), what would they be?

For Your Reference

Industry Glossary

Additional Resources

Recommended Reading

Industry Glossary

Acute care. Treatment of short-term or episodic health problems.

Alternative medicine. See complementary medicine.

Ambulatory care. Medical treatment given on an outpatient basis.

Assisted living. Assisted living provides housing along with services designed for persons requiring assistance with personal care or medications.

Attending physician. The doctor responsible for a patient's treatment and/or billing.

Biofeedback. Biofeedback is a method of consciously controlling a body function that is normally regulated automatically by the body, such as skin temperature, muscle tension, heart rate, or blood pressure.

Ayurveda. Ayurveda is a traditional holistic health system used in India for more than 5,000 years. It emphasizes health promotion and prevention of illness through a wide range of diverse practices (such as meditation, yoga, and dietary changes), beyond simply taking herbal remedies.

Cardiology. The medical study of the heart.

Chiropody. See "Podiatry."

Chronic disease. Ongoing, long-term sickness.

Clinical research organization (CRO). CROs offer a range of development, strategy, and other services for organizations developing new drug therapies.

Complementary medicine. Any treatment that is outside the traditional medicine or practice of your primary health system can be considered complementary medicine. A treatment that is complementary in one culture may be traditional in another. For example, ayurveda is a system of health that has been practiced in India for more than 5,000 years, yet it is considered a complementary medicine in the United States. People often use complementary medicine to improve wellness and quality of life. However, in recent years, more people in the U.S. have been turning to complementary medicine to help manage a wide variety of medical conditions.

Copayment. The portion of a payment for diagnosis or treatment by a health practitioner that the patient, rather than his or her insurance carrier, is responsible for.

Deductible. The amount that a patient must pay for covered health-care services each year before his or her health insurance policy will begin covering the cost of covered care.

Dermatology. The medical study of the skin.

Dietetics. The science of managing food and nutrition to promote health.

Endocrinology. The medical study of the glands and hormones.

Formulary. List of prescription drugs covered by a health insurance plan.

Gastroenterology. The medical study of the stomach, intestines, and associated organs.

Geriatrics. The medical study of the diseases and problems of the elderly.

Hematology. The medical study of the blood and blood-producing organs.

HMO (Health Maintenance Organization). An HMO is a form of health insurance combining a range of coverage on a group basis. A cadre of doctors and other medical professionals offer care through the HMO for a flat monthly rate with no deductibles. However, only visits to professionals within the HMO network are covered by the policy. All visits, prescriptions, and other care must be approved by the HMO in order to be covered. A primary physician within the HMO system manages referrals.

Holistic medicine. See "Complementary."

Home health care. Home health care companies provide home health and adult care products and services, including respiratory therapy, home infusion therapy, home medication, skilled nursing or medical care in the home, and associated home-based services.

In-patient. Admitted at least overnight by a hospital or other health-care facility.

Integrative medicine. See "Complementary."

Informatics. Informatics is another term for "information science," which is the field of study focused on issues related to the management of electronically stored (as well as paper-based) information.

Leapfrog group. A group of large health-care providers which have banded together to use their combined purchasing power to influence health-care services.

Long-term care. Companies that operate care facilities such as assisted living centers, nursing and retirement homes, and various associated health-care services are long-term care providers.

Medicaid. The U.S. federal health insurance program focused on covering the poor.

Medicare. The U.S. federal health insurance program focused on covering the elderly.

Metabolize. To change via physical and chemical processes.

Minimally invasive surgery. Minimally invasive surgery requires fewer incisions than tradition methods. Typically, hospital visits for minimally invasive surgeries are shorter than visits for traditional surgeries. Recovery from minimally invasive surgery is much faster than for traditional surgeries, and the amount of discomfort is reduced.

Morbidity. The rate of incidence of a specific disease within a specific population.

MRI. Magnetic Resonance Imaging (MRI) is a type of testing that employs a magnetic field and pulses of radio wave energy to provide pictures of organs and structures inside the body. In many cases, MRI provides information that cannot be obtained from other methods such as x-ray, ultrasound, or CT scan.

Nephrology. The medical study of the kidneys.

Neurology. The medical study of the nervous system.

NIH (National Institutes of Health). The National Institutes of Health is one of the world's foremost medical research centers. The NIH comprises 27 separate institutes and centers. Their mission is to discover ways to help prevent, detect, diagnose, and treat disease and disability—from the rarest genetic disorder to the common cold.

Naturopathy. Naturopathy (naturopathic medicine) is a philosophy based on the belief that the body can heal itself and that treatments should support normal body functions. By promoting the concepts deriving from other areas of complementary medicine (such as ayurveda, homeopathy, and herbal therapies), naturopathic medicine works to enhance and maintain quality of health; it also treats and prevents diseases. The goal of naturopathy is to help people become well and stay well, which is believed to be the natural state of the body.

Obstetrics. The medical study of pregnancy and childbirth.

Oncology. The medical study of cancer.

Ophthalmology. The medical study of the eyes.

Orthopedics. The medical study of the skeletal system and associated muscles, ligaments, and joints.

Osteopathy. A medical system based on the belief that problems in the musculoskeletal system cause health problems in other parts of the body.

Otology. The medical study of the ear.

Outpatient. A patient treated in a hospital or other health-care facility who does not require an overnight stay.

Pediatrics. The medical study of the diseases and treatment of the young.

Podiatry. The medical study of the foot.

POS (Point of Service). A hybrid of sorts, the point of service plan mixes the flexibility of a PPO with the lower cost of an HMO.

PPO (Preferred Provider Organization). A PPO is a health-care organization composed of physicians, hospitals, or other providers which offers health-care services at a reduced rate.

Public health. Public health is the field of study concerning the monitoring and influencing of trends in both habits and disease toward the goal of safeguarding or enhancing the health of a particular population.

Radiology. The medical study of the use of radioactive substances in the diagnosis and treatment of health-care problems. Among other things, radiologists take x-rays.

Referral. The recommendation by a primary care practitioner that a patient see another practitioner, usually a specialist in whatever's ailing the patient.

Rheumatology. The study of pathologies of the muscles, tendons, joints, bones, or nerves.

Regional Health Care Information Organizations (RHIOs). In an effort to cut costs, these RHIOs (decentralized networks of outpatient care) were set up in the late 1980s to enable better information technology access for under-served communities.

Specialty provider. Specialty providers offer niche health-care services such as kidney dialysis, rehabilitation, intensive care, mental health care, and the likes.

Stem cells. Stem cells are immature, undifferentiated cells having the potential to grow into any one of the body's cell types. Embryonic stem cells are most often employed in research, while adult stem cells are applied in the treatment of disease.

Telemedicine. The use of telecommunications technology to facilitate medical diagnosis and treatment.

Triage. The assessment of patients' conditions and prioritization of patients' need for care.

Wellness. A state of good physical, mental, and social health or way of life that facilitates good health.

Additional Resources

ONLINE RESOURCES

A Chance to Cut is a Chance to Cure (www.cut-to-cure.blogspot.com)
A perspective on medical and other issues from a general surgeon.

ADVANCE for Health Information Professionals
(http://health-information.advanceweb.com)
News, vendor listings, jobs, etc. for health-information professionals.

AMA Health Professions page (www.ama-assn.org/ama/pub/category/14598.html)
PDF downloads containing information about various medical careers.

BCBSHealthIssues.com (bcbshealthissues.com)
Published by the Blue Cross and Blue Shield Association, this site features news relating
to public policy and health-care insurance coverage.

Careers in Healthcare Management (www.healthmanagementcareers.org)
This site, run by the American College of Healthcare Executives, provides information
on careers in health-care management and administration.

DB's Medical Rants (www.medrants.com)
Blog covering medicine and the health-care system.

GruntDoc (http://gruntdoc.com)
Blog of an emergency physician practicing in Texas.

Health Care Careers (www.waycoolsurgery.com/careers/index.shtml)
Website with information on health-care careers in biomedical engineering, emergency
medical services, laboratory settings, medical records, nursing, nutrition services, pharmacy, radiology, rehabilitation services, and respiratory therapy.

Health Management Technology (www.healthmgttech.com)
Health care IT management magazine.

HealthWeb (www.healthweb.org)
Database of health-care websites.

Knowledge@Wharton Health Economics page
(http://knowledge.wharton.upenn.edu/index.cfm?fa=viewCat&CID=6)
Covering health-care business and strategy issues.

Managed Care (www.managedcaremag.com)
A guide for managed care executives and physicians covering capitation, compensation, disease management, accreditation, contracting, ethics, practice management, formulary development, and other health insurance issues.

McKinsey Quarterly Health Care page
(www.mckinseyquarterly.com/category_editor.aspx?L2=12&srid=6)
In-depth analysis of health care business issues.

MedCareers (www.medcareers.com)
Medical careers website.

Medpundit (http://medpundit.blogspot.com)
Commentary on medical news by a practicing physician.

Modern Healthcare (www.modernhealthcare.com)
Site run by Crain Communications, a business publisher, covering health-care industry news and issues.

Monster.com's MedSearch page (www.medsearch.com)
Monster's health care–related site, MedSearch is packed with job listings and information about careers in health care.

National Center for Health Statistics (www.cdc.gov/nchs/)
All the health care–related data you could ever want.

New England Journal of Medicine (content.neim.org/)
The online presence of the noted medical journal.

over my med body (www.grahamazon.com/)
Blog by third-year med student.

RNWeb (www.rnweb.com)
Website of *RN* magazine.

The Health Care Blog (www.thehealthcareblog.com)
Must-read blog by industry consultant Matthew Holt.

The Healthcare IT Guy (www.healthcareguy.com)
Blog by a longtime health care IT professional.

PROFESSIONAL ASSOCIATIONS

Alliance of Cardiovascular Professionals (www.acp-online.org)

American Academy of Anesthesiologists' Assistants (www.anesthetist.org)

American Academy of Nurse Practitioners (www.aanp.org)

American Academy of Physician Assistants (www.aapa.org)

American Art Therapy Association (www.arttherapy.org)

American Association for Respiratory Care (www.aarc.org)

American Association for Medical Transcription (www.aamt.org)

American Association of Colleges of Nursing (www.aacn.nche.edu)

American Association of Colleges of Pharmacy (www.aacp.org)

American Association of Colleges of Podiatric Medicine (www.aacpm.org)

American Association of Critical-Care Nurses (www.aacn.org)

American Association of Medical Assistants (www.aama-ntl.org)

American Association of Medical Dosimetrists (www.medicaldosimetry.org)

American Association of Naturalpathic Physicians (www.naturopathic.org)

American Association of Pathologists' Assistants (www.pathologistsassistants.org)

American Association of Pharmacy Technicians (www.pharmacytechnician.com)

American Counseling Association (www.counseling.org)

American Dental Assistants Association (www.dentalassistant.org)

American Dental Association (www.ada.org)

American Dental Hygienists' Association (www.adha.org)

American Dietetic Association (www.eatright.org)

American Health Information Management Association (ahima.org)

American Kinesiotherapy Association (www.akta.org)

American Medical Association (www.ama-assn.org)

American Medical Students Association (www.amsa.org)

American Music Therapy Association (www.musictherapy.org)

American Nurses Association (www.ana.org)

American Nursing Informatics Association (www.ania.org)

American Occupational Therapy Association (www.aota.org)

American Orthoptic Council (www.orthoptics.org)

American Orthotic and Prosthetic Association (www.aopanet.org)

American Physical Therapy Association (www.apta.org)

American Society for Clinical Laboratory Science (www.ascls.org)

American Society for Clinical Pathology (www.ascp.org)

American Society of Anesthesia Technologists and Technicians (www.asatt.org)

American Society of Cytopathology (www.cytopathology.org)

American Society of Echocardiography (www.asecho.org)

American Society of Electroneurodiagnostic Technologists (www.aset.org)

American Society of Extra-Corporeal Technologists (www.amsect.org)

American Society of Radiologic Technologists (www.asrt.org)

American Speech-Language-Hearing Association (www.asha.org)

American Therapeutic Recreation Association (www.atra-tr.org)

Association for Education and Rehabilitation of the Blind and Visually Impaired (www.aerbvi.org)

Association of American Medical Colleges (www.aamc.org)

Association of Genetic Technologists (www.agt-info.org)

Association of Polysomnographic Technologists (www.aptweb.org)

Association of Surgical Technologists (www.ast.org)

Healthcare Financial Management Association (www.hfma.org)

Joint Commission on Allied Health Personnel in Opthalmology (www.jcahpo.org/newsite/index.htm)

National Accrediting Agency for Clinical Laboratory Sciences (www.naacls.org)

National Association of Dental Laboratories (www.nadl.org)

National Association of Emergency Medical Technicians (www.naemt.org)

National Athletic Trainers' Association (www.nata.org)

National League for Nursing (www.nln.org)

National Rehabilitation Counseling Association (http://nrca-net.org)

National Society of Genetic Counselors (www.nsgc.org)

National Society for Histotechnology (www.nsh.org)

National Surgical Assistant Association (www.nsaa.net)

Optical Laboratories Association (www.ola-labs.org)

Society of Diagnostic Medical Sonographers (www.sdms.org)

Society of Nuclear Medicine—Technologist Section (www.snm.org)

Society for Vascular Ultrasound (www.svunet.org)

Recommended Reading

BOOKS

A Brief History of Disease, Science, and Medicine
(Michael Kennedy, Asklepiad Press, 2004)

This book covers everything from prehistoric times to the present day, with an emphasis on 20th century developments.

Alternatives in Healing: An Open-minded Approach to Finding the Best Treatment for Your Health Problems
(Simon Mills, MA and Steven J. Finando, Ph.D., New Amercian Library, 1988)

An open-minded assessment of various alternative health-care modalities. A no-nonsense guide to healing utilizing ancient, yet time-proven methods.

Anyone, Anything, Anytime: A History of Emergency Medicine
(Brian Zink, Mosby Elsevier, 2005)

A look at the evolution of emergency medicine.

Beyond Managed Care: How Consumers and Technology Are Changing the Future of Health Care
(Dean C. Coddington, Elizabeth A. Fischer, Keith D. Moore, and Richard L. Clarke, Jossey-Bass, 2000)

A look at how things like the Internet and clinical information technology are changing the shape of the health-care industry.

The Cambridge Illustrated History of Medicine
(Roy Porter, ed., Cambridge University Press, 2001)

A study of medical history in a variety of cultures.

The Care of Strangers: The Rise of America's Hospital System
(Charles E. Rosenberg, The Johns Hopkins University Press, 1995)

The history and evolution of hospitals in the United States.

Choose the Right Long-Term Care: Home Care, Assisted Living & Nursing Homes
(Nolo Press, 4th edition, 2002)

Although this guide was written expressly for those seeking home-care services, the same clear and succinct exposition and diligence that are Nolo's claim to fame will help those investigating the career field. Various jobs in the field are described in this book.

Complications: A Surgeon's Notes on an Imperfect Science
(Atul Gawande, Picador, 2003)

An insider's tales of life in the surgery trenches.

The Economic Evolution of American Health Care: From Marcus Welby to Managed Care
(David Dranove, Princeton University Press, 2002)

An in-depth look at the historical evolution of health-care technology and economics.

Healthwise Handbook
(Healthwise, Inc., Boise, ID, 2003)

Kaiser Permanente's famous book on preventative medicine and self-care, which is given to all new members. Based on the philosophy that educated people are much better patients, this book is a health care how-to guide for the whole family.

Managed Care: What It Is and How It Works (Second Edition)
(Peter R. Kongstvedt, Aspen Publishers, 2003)

A look at the history and current state of managed care.

Medicare's Midlife Crisis
(Sue A. Blevins, Cato Institute, 2001)

All about Medicare's history, administration, and effects on patients and society.

On Call: A Doctor's Days and Nights in Residency
(Emily Transue, St. Martin's Press, 2004)

The story of one young doctor's internal medicine residency.

Professional Guide to Complementary and Alternative Therapies
(Springhouse Corporation, Lippincott Williams & Wilkins, 2001)

Acupuncture to osteopathy to Ayurvedic medicine and more.

Social Transformation of American Medicine
(Paul Starr, Basic Books, 1984)

Pulitzer Prize–winning book tracing the history of health care in America.

WETFEET'S INSIDER GUIDE SERIES

Job Search Guides

Getting Your Ideal Internship

Job Hunting A to Z: Landing the Job You Want

Killer Consulting Resumes!

Killer Cover Letters & Resumes!

Killer Investment Banking Resumes!

Negotiating Your Salary & Perks

Networking Works!

The International MBA Student's Guide to the U.S. Job Search

Interview Guides

Ace Your Case: Consulting Interviews

Ace Your Case II: 15 More Consulting Cases

Ace Your Case III: Practice Makes Perfect

Ace Your Case IV: The Latest & Greatest

Ace Your Case V: Return to the Case Interview

Ace Your Case VI: Mastering the Case Interview

Ace Your Interview!

Beat the Street: Investment Banking Interviews

Beat the Street II: I-Banking Interview Practice Guide

Career & Industry Guides

Careers in Accounting

Careers in Advertising & Public Relations

Careers in Asset Management & Retail Brokerage

Careers in Biotech & Pharmaceuticals

Careers in Brand Management

Careers in Consumer Products

Careers in Entertainment & Sports

Careers in Health Care

Careers in Human Resources

Careers in Information Technology

Careers in Investment Banking

Careers in Management Consulting

Careers in Marketing & Market Research

Careers in Nonprofits & Government Agencies

Careers in Real Estate

Careers in Retail

Careers in Sales

Careers in Supply Chain Management

Careers in Venture Capital

Industries & Careers for MBAs

Industries & Careers for Undergrads

Million Dollar Careers

Specialized Consulting Careers: Health Care, Human Resources, and Information Technology

Company Guides

25 Top Consulting Firms

25 Top Financial Services Firms

Accenture

Bain & Company

Booz Allen Hamilton

Boston Consulting Group

Credit Suisse First Boston

Deloitte Consulting

Deutsche Bank

The Goldman Sachs Group

J.P. Morgan Chase & Co.

McKinsey & Company

Merrill Lynch & Co.

Morgan Stanley

WetFeet in the City Guides

Job Hunting in New York City

Job Hunting in San Francisco